ATHEISTS

Bruce E. Hunsberger

and

Bob Altemeyer

ATHEISTS

A Groundbreaking
Study of
America's Nonbelievers

Prometheus Books

59 John Glenn Drive
Amherst, New York 14228-2197

Published 2006 by Prometheus Books

Inquiries should be addressed to
Prometheus Books
59 John Glenn Drive
Amherst, New York 14228–2197
VOICE: 716–691–0133, ext. 207
FAX: 716–564–2711
WWW.PROMETHEUSBOOKS.COM

10 09 08 07 06   5 4 3 2 1

Library of Congress Cataloging-in-Publication Data

Hunsberger, Bruce E.
     Atheists : a groundbreaking study of America's nonbelievers / Bruce E. Hunsberger and Bob Altemeyer.
          p. cm.
     Includes bibliographical references and index.
     ISBN-13: 978–1–59102–413–2 (pbk. : alk. paper)
     ISBN-10: 1–59102–413–7 (pbk. : alk. paper)
     1. Atheism—United States. I. Altemeyer, Bob, 1940– II. Title.

BL2760.H86 2006
211'.80973—dc22

2006008265

Printed in the United States of America on acid-free paper

Dedicated to the joyous memory of Bruce Hunsberger.

CONTENTS

ACKNOWLEDGMENTS

O nly one of us is left. Bruce Hunsberger, my co-researcher and best friend, died in October 2003 from the leukemia he had bravely battled for over a decade. Everyone who knew Bruce thanked and cherished every day he was with us. That was especially true of the "Alts." Our families were close, even though we lived a thousand miles apart. Times together provided enormous fun, a highlight of any year for everybody. The only dark spot on these gatherings occurred when Bruce and I began talking research. Then everyone else would groan and leave the room. Or make us leave. So mainly we talked research via e-mail almost every day we were not together. This book is the last project we did.

Bruce and his wife, Emily, told Jean and me about his illness in May 1994 while we four were spending a short visit in one of our favorite places, San Francisco. He assured us he would last at least until the visit was over, that in fact he had at least five years to live, but he knew sooner or later his illness would claim him. Time and chemotherapies and recoveries passed, but he and Emily always hoped for "one last good spell." He made me a promise in his last year: if there was an afterlife, he said, he would do everything he could to let me know. It would be a great surprise ending for a book about atheists, he observed. I haven't heard from him yet, however, so it would seem the question remains open.

Bruce and I always fought over who should be the first author of our papers and books. Bruce always won, and I have always been the first author. His clinching argument was inevitably that if the names were in alphabetical order, it would not necessarily mean anything about who deserved the greater credit or blame. So as we were having this fight again over the book in your hands, I made him a bet. I would agree to be first author if he would stay alive until the book was published. Otherwise he was going to be first author and there wouldn't be anything he could do about it. I thought I had him trapped. I was proved wrong.

While I am praising people for their willingness to face unpleasant truths with courage, I want to draw attention to the agents at each end of this production. This research project began when a member of an atheists club in the San Francisco area, Chris Lindstrom, read the book Bruce and I wrote in 1997 about religious conversion and religious abandonment. She offered to help us do a study of atheists in the Bay Area. We never thought anyone would volunteer "her kind" to be put under a microscope like that, for Chris knew we would ask the tough questions and let the answers fall where they may. But Chris did and when the wrinkles and warts turned up in the data, her basic reaction was, "It's best to be seen as we are, even if it's not like what we want to be."

At the other end of this story we find Prometheus Books, undoubtedly the leading publisher of skeptical material in North America, if not the world. I imagine you would find many atheists aboard Prometheus, from the board of directors through the editors to the staff. When they picked up the manuscript they may have thought, "Hot dog, a book that's going to show what great people atheists are!" There is good news for atheists in this book, but when the editors got to the central chapters they must have been dismayed at what some of the numbers said. Still, they wanted to publish the book. I think you can say they are committed to the truth, whatever it is, and I don't have much higher praise for someone than that. They deserve a "Bruce Award."

Steven L. Mitchell championed this book at Prometheus and agreed to a special feature of this book, which is responses of some of the atheists who participated in this study. You'll find their feedback on our feedback in the last chapter. Additionally, some unknown person found a way, despite Bill Gates's best efforts, to get the manuscript from my WordPerfect into Prometheus's Word. ("Oh! Icky!" said Word.) Mark Hall had the thankless job of trying to get me to help market the book. Christine Kramer served as production manager, a person with almost infinite power to make a book attractive and readable, or else "academic." Then there was Jeremy Sauer, the editor assigned to do battle with me over my "relaxed" writing style and alarming ignorance of grammar. Mary Read took over when Jeremy took another position toward the end of the editing—which I am assured was not my fault.

Allen Patterson of Information Services and Technology at the University of Manitoba configured and reconfigured and configured some more the charts in this book until I finally figured out what I wanted them to show.

Which brings up one last salute to Bruce. The only other thing we fought about besides order of authorship was how many dozen commas to put in a sentence. Bruce thought the more commas the better, even if they came in the middle of words or there were no words at all. I on the other hand have always believed that if you give the reader a chance to pause he may just put the book down and never finish it. So we would send each other's versions of a manuscript back and forth with millions of "inserts" and "deletes"—all about commas. I even considered hiring a composer to develop a "Fanfare for the Comma Man" for Bruce.

Well old buddy, you win. The editors have been on your side all the way, and this book contains way, way more commas than I would like. Let's, hope, people, keep, reading, it, any, way. ,,,,,,,,,,

INTRODUCTION

T his book is about quite unusual people. It focuses on individuals who have reached a very different conclusion from most people about the basic question of life; they have firmly concluded there is no God, no supernatural being of any kind. Nothing.

A solid majority of North Americans believe in God, according to the polls. A few folks, like the authors of this book, say they honestly do not know and are called agnostics. And every now and then you come across an atheist, who positively says the negative—there is no God. If you have never met an atheist, pull up a chair. If you know one or two, and want to see what other atheists are like, have a look. And if *you* are an atheist and would like to know what we discovered in our studies of other atheists, read on.

These investigations may prove particularly interesting because for the most part we have studied active atheists—people who have joined atheists clubs just as one might join a reading club or a gourmet group. Of course, some of our informants do nothing more "active" than read the club newsletter. But some really energetic atheists have had dramatic impacts on our society. Madalyn Murray O'Hair played a leading role in the court cases that abolished prayer and scripture reading in American public schools. Michael Newdow is trying to remove "under God" from the Pledge of Allegiance. The American Atheists Association is urging its members to cross out the phrase "In God we trust" on American currency. Blair Scott and other atheists helped file the lawsuit that removed the Ten Commandments monument from the Alabama state judicial building. In Butch Cassidy's words, "Who are those guys?"

THE DECLINE OF ORGANIZED RELIGION IN THE WEST

Whether you are a theist, an agnostic, or an atheist, the question above deserves our attention because organized religion seems to be dying in most of the Judeo-

Christian world. The "unreligious" are swelling in number faster than any religious group—including the Protestant fundamentalists who *appear* to be making big gains in some places. Parents in most Western countries seldom take their children to church any more, so the odds are their grandchildren won't go either. Why is this happening? We shall poke and probe.

It might surprise many Americans that religion is dying in the Western world. But in European countries where different faiths once ignited ferocious wars, few care any more. In nations where church and state were once so intertwined that kings made bishops and bishops made kings, the national religion cannot block Sunday shopping. In places where clerics once burned books, and opponents, religion does not even bother to classify movies any more. Mullahs and ayatollahs may wield enormous power over their faithful, but the sun has set on clerical power in most Western countries because the faithful are few and far between in the community. Once-packed churches draw handfuls of worshipers on Sundays now. And the synagogues have emptied as well.

What is the evidence for these bald assertions? An organization of social scientists named the International Social Survey Program conducted a massive survey on religion using representative samples from thirty countries in 1998–1999. Nothing else comes close to giving a same-time, same-methodology, same-questions snapshot of religious behavior and beliefs in different nations. You can look up the study at http://www.gesis.org/en/data_service/issp/data/1998_Religion_II.htm.

Question V218 on the survey asked, "How often do you attend religious services?" People's answers ranged from "Daily" to "Never." Looking at Europe first, how many Britons do you think said they go to church at least weekly, or nearly weekly? Just 14 percent. How many do you think said they rarely or never go? Seventy-six percent. (The remaining 10 percent said they attend one to three times per month.) Remember Henry VIII, Elizabeth I, and all those beheadings and religious wars? Very few Britons care enough about religion nowadays to even go to church. (See table 1.)

What about Germany, home of Martin Luther, the Reformation, and Protestant-Catholic strife? Christian fervor hardly fills the pews, much less fields of battle now. In former East Germany, only 7 percent go weekly, and 75 percent rarely/never go. Well sure, but that's because of godless Communism's influence on a whole generation, right? Maybe not. In former West Germany, the figures came in at 8 percent and 74 percent, respectively. (Godless capitalism?)

France? 12 percent versus 84 percent. The Netherlands? 14 percent versus 76 percent. Switzerland, 12 percent versus 74 percent. Scandinavia, land of state religions and dark Ingmar Bergman movies about oppressive Lutheran dominance: 6 percent versus 92 percent in Sweden, 6 percent versus 90 percent in Norway, 2 percent versus 89 percent in Denmark. Great Britain positively swarms with churchgoers by comparison.

Surely attendance is higher in the Catholic countries. Yes it is. In fact in Ireland most people (63 percent) said they go to church weekly, and only 22 percent rarely/never. But Ireland is the only country in all of Europe where a majority

Table 1
Results of the 1998–99 International Social Survey Program "Religion II" Study.

Question: "How often do you attend religious services?"

Country	% Weekly or More[a]	% Never or Rarely[b]
Australia	18	75
Austria	19	67
Canada	20	67
Chile	20	55
Cyprus	4	75
Czechoslovakia	7	85
Denmark	2	89
France	12	84
Germany, East	7	75
Germany, West	8	74
Great Britain	14	76
Hungary	15	76
Ireland	63	22
Italy	29	51
Japan	2	93
Latvia	5	81
Netherlands	14	76
New Zealand	13	76
Northern Ireland	44	41
Norway	6	90
Philippines	46	26
Poland	39	29
Portugal	30	53
Russia	4	91
Slovakia	30	55
Slovenia	13	73
Spain	27	57
Sweden	6	92
Switzerland	12	74
United States	32	52

[a]Compiled by adding the responses "Nearly Every Week," "Once a Week," and "More Than Once a Week."

[b]Compiled by adding the responses "Never," "Less Than Once Per Year," and "Several Times a Year." The table thus omits indications of "Once a Month" and "Two to Three Times a Month."

These data, which have been rounded to the nearest percent, were reported by the International Social Survey Program: Religion II, 1998, produced by Zentralarchiv fuer Empirische Sozialforschung (Koeln, Germany), 2000, pp. 182–83.

attends so "faithfully." In Italy the figures were 29 percent versus 51 percent; in Spain, 27 percent versus 57 percent; in Portugal, 30 percent versus 53 percent. In Poland at least more people said they go to church weekly (39 percent) than rarely (29 percent)—but still most people do not attend every week. To the south, in the Czech Republic, the pollsters reported 7 percent versus 85 percent; in Slovakia, 30 percent versus 55 percent; in Slovenia, 13 percent versus 73 percent; in Hungary, 15 percent versus 76 percent; and in Austria, 19 percent versus 67 percent.

One of us remembers praying after every Sunday Mass as a youth for the conversion of Russia (that is, to Catholicism). Those prayers have yet to be answered, and it will be quite a battle, with 4 percent versus 91 percent.

THE UNITED STATES AND CANADA

Hopping the Atlantic, what did the ISSP survey find in North America? The United States proved one of the most religious countries in the survey, with 32 percent saying they attended church regularly. Nevertheless, most (52 percent) of the American sample said they never or seldom went. In Canada, where the authors happen to live, the numbers came in 20 percent versus 67 percent.

This all splices into a larger story of how American and Canadian cultures have grown apart, as demonstrated by Michael Adams in his 2003 book, *Fire and Ice*. Fifty years ago Canada needed large churches to accommodate the faithful, as 60 percent of its adults attended services regularly—compared to 50 percent of Americans at that time.[1] Attendance seems to have dropped in both countries since, but considerably more in Canada where many of those places of worship now seem cavernously empty week in and week out.[2] Then was then, this is now. Canada has become markedly less religious than the United States.

By one set of data, in fact, American church attendance has not dropped at all. A Gallup poll found that 41 percent of its 1939 sample said they had gone to services in the last week—a question that combines regular and occasional attenders on any given week—and that figure has basically held true ever since. But another big study, the General Social Survey by the National Opinion Research Center (www.icpsr.umich.edu:8080/GSS/homepage.htm), has asked the ISSP question about the frequency of service attendance, and it found a drop in weekly (or better) attendance from 41 percent in its first poll in 1972 to 33 percent in 2004. So *regular* church attendance has apparently been dropping in the United States, but much more slowly than in Canada and elsewhere.

BUT AREN'T THE FUNDAMENTALISTS GROWING?

Many people, noticing jammed parking lots, bumper stickers that say "Jesus Is the Answer," and the 2004 American election, believe fundamentalist Protestant denominations are growing by leaps and bounds in North America. But the polls tell a somewhat different story. The number of people in Canada who say they are "conservative" Protestants *has* increased over the years, but it has also remained about 8 percent of the likewise growing Canadian population since 1871.[3] One finds far more conservatives in the United States, but the General Social Survey reveals that the number of Americans who call themselves fundamentalists (as opposed to "moderates" or "liberals") peaked at 36 percent in 1987, and has since dropped to 30 percent in 2004.[4]

If you're wondering which group has been growing, it's the people who tell pollsters they belong to no religion, the "Nones," who went from 5 percent of the general population in the 1972 General Social Survey in the United States to 14 percent in 1998—a figure they held in 2000, 2002, and 2004.

The authors of this book can provide a more detailed look at this trend in an admittedly less representative population, namely *parents* of introductory psychology students at the University of Manitoba. Over the last ten years more than five thousand of them have answered a question about the religion they were raised in, and another asking their present religious affiliation. The number of "Nones" skyrocketed in that decade nearly 300 percent (from 270 raised that way to 1,003 who call themselves that now). By comparison, the number of fundamentalist Protestants went up just 18 percent (from 314 to 372)—although they constitute by far the most active, church-attending segment of the sample.[5] So the real story in shifting religious affiliation has been the growth in apostasy—primarily at the expense of the mainline religions. But you notice this less because people who stay home on Sundays fill garages, not parking lots, they do not attend movies such as *The Passion of the Christ* en masse, and for some reason they shy away from displaying bumper stickers proclaiming "Jesus Is NOT the Answer."

WHY HAS APOSTASY INCREASED SO MUCH?

Why have the Nones grown so much? Ironically, partly because the fundamentalists drove them away. Michael Hout and Claude S. Fischer concluded in 2002 from analyses of poll data that the rise in apostasy in the United States has occurred primarily among persons with weak ties to organized religion who have been driven from their faith by the behavior of the "religious right."[6] We found a similar backlash when studying why attitudes toward homosexuals have generally become more positive in a short period of time. Manitoba students and their parents both gave as one of the principal reasons for their shifts, "I have been turned off by antihomosexual people."[7] If your community is like ours, the most vocal opposition to laws protecting gays has come from fundamentalists. (We shall find further evidence of such a backlash later in this book.)

We explored this drift from organized religion with a 1999 survey of Manitoba parents who had stressed the family religion less to their children than it had been stressed to them as they were growing up. They were asked whether any of fourteen possible factors had led them to *not* "pass it on" (table 2). They could rate each factor anywhere from 0 (it had no effect at all) to 6 (it had influenced them to a great extent). You can see that all of the reasons had been a factor for some people. For many, their own religious training had fallen on hard ground. For many, church proved boring. For many, the teachings didn't make sense. Or the church seemed preoccupied with money. And so on. But the reason cited most often, and the thing that had walloped church affiliation the most, was that the parent had spotted hypocrisy among the faithful.

We asked for more details of this other kind of "witnessing" in a follow-up study. Usually, parents said, the hypocrisy appeared among members of the congregation, although the clergy were named often too. The most common examples involved "the holy people" looking down on others in the community, particularly regarding wealth, status, and dress in church, being "Sunday-only Christians," being judgmental, and being prejudiced. Usually these hypocrisies had been spotted when the parent had been a teenager. As the parents were now typically in their late forties, the hypocrisy obviously had a lasting effect.[8]

WILL THE SHIFT TO "NONES" CONTINUE?

Look again at item 14 in table 2, the one about social norms. While it pulled down a relatively hefty average score, most social psychologists would probably suspect it was even more powerful, that is, that changing social norms played a strong role in cutting church attendance. People seldom realize how much they are affected by what others are doing. For generations a large part of the community went to church, with their children, thinking, "that's what good people do." But as the pews get emptier and emptier, the perception inevitably grows in anyone who looks around that lots of people don't believe this anymore. And the more folks who stop going, the weaker the norm becomes until . . . Hello Europe?

Will church attendance and affiliation decrease yet more? It certainly has in the current crop of students at the University of Manitoba, who go to church less than their parents did as young adults, and who know little about the Bible other than it usually has a black cover.[9] Why are they so disinterested? Many of their parents—the inheritors of a family religion passed down for generations—stopped going to church themselves many years ago. What are the odds that their children will find religion, crack open that dusty family Bible, and take *their* children to services?

It does happen. About a third of our parent samples who received no religious training as children say they now belong to a religion. But ten times as many started off in a religion and became Nones. When we asked today's middle-aged apostates if they will ever go back, some said they might as death nears or if a personal disaster strikes them. But most said no.[10] They may tell census-takers that they are Anglicans, Catholics, or whatever, they may still be on the church rolls and suck up

Table 2
Possible Reasons for Parents' Emphasizing the Family Religion Less to Their Children

Average Item

2.70   1. My own religious training ultimately did not "take." I do not believe most of the things I was taught.

2.92   2. Church was boring. I wanted to do other things with my time.

2.73   3. The religious teachings I was taught seem contradictory and don't make much sense; I didn't want to pass them on.

2.77   4. My partner's attitudes toward religion led me to emphasize religion less to our children.

2.22   5. My child resisted religious traiing; I tried, but s/he just wasn't that interested.

2.88   6. The church seemed preoccupied with getting money from us; that turned me off.

2.59   7. Work schedules (late Saturday night or Sunday morning) interfered with getting our kids to church.

2.36   8. I had unpleasant personal experiences/conflicts with religious officials.

2.43   9. My child's Sunday morning activities, such as sports, interfered with getting to church.

2.46   10. Tragedies such as illness and death led me to question my religion's teachings.

2.77   11. I could not agree with certain important teachings of my religion.

3.08   12. As I grew up, I saw a lot of hypocrisy in the people in my religion.

2.60   13. The teachings of my religion seemed less and less relevant to the problems of our day.

2.88   14. In my youth, if you did not go to church, pray, etc. people thought there was something wrong with you. It's not like that anymore.

Note: The statements were answered on a 0–6 basis. The figures given as the averages are arithmetic means.

part of the parish postage budget, but they only enter the building for marrying and burying, and do not help pay the heating bills.

Some lost sheep anticipate rejoining the flock if disaster strikes them, so perhaps a major calamity could fill the churches again. What happened after September 11, 2001, in the United States? According to a Gallup poll, church attendance jumped a little right after the attack, from 41 percent to 47 percent. But by November the numbers had seeped down to their pre–9/11 levels.[11] Of course, by November 2001 most Americans probably felt safer than they did right after the September 11 terrorist attack. Bring on a hurtling asteroid, bring in massive economic ruin, bring back the plague, and the clergy may have to lay on extra services. Even in Sweden. But apparently it will take something really big and sustained. For all that had happened, for all the uncertainty, most Americans apparently still did *not* go to church on Sunday, September 16, 2001.

BUT SOME NONES MAY BE "RELIGIOUS"

Thus far we have been talking about organized religions, and they seem to be declining, and to be massively declined, in most Western countries. But people can be "religious" in many ways besides identifying with a faith and attending services. Many persons who seldom go to church tell the pollsters that they nonetheless believe in God, believe in an afterlife, and pray at least weekly. In the big ISSP and GSS polls we have been discussing, between 70 and 80 percent of Americans said they do. In Canada the figures turn up closer to 60 percent. In Europe these personal beliefs range from a pronounced majority (about 80 percent in Ireland) to a distinct minority (Germany: 28 percent, Scandinavia: 33 percent). But everywhere more people believe in God and an afterlife than go to church. So private religiousness has not disappeared to nearly the extent that the congregations have. Organized religion has taken a big-time hit; personal beliefs, much less so.

NOT ALL OF THE NONES ARE ATHEISTS

If some Nones thus continue to hold some traditional religious beliefs, how many go the other way and do not believe in God, a God, any God, at all? Not many. Atheists, the subjects of this book, are pretty scarce in most places. In the 1998–1999 ISSP Religion II Study that found 14 percent of the American public called themselves Nones, only 3 percent said they positively did not believe in God. Atheism turned up three times as often in Canada, but that still only amounts to 9 percent. European rates usually top North American levels. Where should you go in Europe if you want to buy a random stranger a glass of wine and find yourself discussing life with an atheist? Besides most ex-Communist countries, France (19 percent), Sweden (17 percent), The Netherlands (17 percent), Denmark (15 percent), Norway

(12 percent), West Germany (12 percent), and Great Britain (10 percent) give you your best chance. But as you can see from the numbers, even in these places it will cost you five to ten glasses of wine on average to find an atheist. Clearly, countries where organized religion has fallen on hard times have "lots" of atheists, but even then you do not really find crowds of them.[12]

You also do not find a lot of existing research on atheists. Social scientists have studied religion intensively, from the relation between psychedelic drugs and religious experiences to the tendency of religious women to avoid topless beaches in Australia. But one finds virtually no systematic objective studies of atheists. When we consulted PsychINFO—an abstracting service that lists just about every journal article, book, or doctoral dissertation that might be even loosely related to psychology—we found lots of philosophical, psychoanalytic, and other "arm chair" reflections on atheism. Want to know if someone thinks people become atheists because they unconsciously doubted that their mothers loved them? Want to read someone's notion that atheism is related to sexuality? Ever wonder if, in someone's view, Alcoholics Anonymous can help atheists? You can find opinions on these matters in the literature. But if you want to know what a sample of atheists thinks, or how they score on some objective personality tests, or if they dislike some highly religious people as much as some highly religious people dislike them, we could not find a thing. Want to see a hypothesis about atheists that got empirically tested? It must have happened, but we did not find any examples in the psychological literature.

You won't do any better if you search the sociological records. To be sure, atheists have been *included* in analyses of "unbelievers" (which would also include agnostics) or "the nonreligious" (which might be garnished with unaffiliated theists as well) or "non-attenders" (which might include the lapsed Catholic next door). But we simply could not find an objective empirical study that focused on atheists.

So read on. We may not be heading where angels fear to tread, but we do seem to be going where no one has gone before.

NOTES

1. Michael Adams, *Fire and Ice: The United States, Canada and the Myth of Converging Values* (Toronto, ON: Penguin Books, 2003), p. 50.

2. Reginald W. Bibby, *Restless Gods* (Toronto, ON: Stoddart, 2002), pp. 72–73.

3. Canadian sociologist Reginald Bibby depicts a similar decline in Canadian church attendance in *Restless Gods* (p. 13), except he used Gallup poll answers to the somewhat different inquiry, "Did you yourself happen to attend church or synagogue in the last seven days, or not?" The percentage dropped from 70 percent to 35 percent from 1945 to 1985 in the Gallup data—about 1 percent per year. Such slow but steady erosion chisels away at religion over the decades. Bibby had better news for the churches in his 2004 book, *Restless Churches* (Toronto, ON: Novalis Press), p. 23, reporting a 2003 poll had found 26 percent of Canadian adults say they are attending services approximately once a week—up substantially from his own finding of 21 percent in 2000. But a 2003 Ipsos-Reid poll found only 19 percent of a rep-

resentative Canadian sample said they attended religious services or meetings once a week, or more, during the past year. An Ipsos-Reid poll released in April 2006 reported only 17 percent of Canadians now say they go to church regularly.

4. But didn't George Bush win reelection in 2004 because of the growth in the religious conservative vote? Yes he did, and it well illustrates the power that organized religion has in the United States to shape the country's future. But the president's chief campaign strategist, Karl Rove, famously targeted four million existing "evangelicals" who did not vote in 2000, not four million new converts to the "religious right." Another crucial success of the Republicans' "faith and values campaign" was the successful wooing of the Catholic vote, which went Democratic in 2000 by a 50 percent to 46 percent margin, but Republican in 2004 by 52 percent to 47 percent. George Barna, who regularly uses representative samples to track religious affiliation and other variables in the United States, observed in 2005 that "for more than a decade the sizes of the born-again and (not born-again) segments have been roughly equivalent" (http://www.barna.org/FlexPage.aspx?Page=BarnaUpdate & BarnaUpdate).

5. The fundamentalist Protestant sects were the only faiths to *increase* in numbers among the Manitoba parents from home religion to present religion, demonstrating their success at winning converts from other denominations. They *had* to gain a lot of converts to offset their own losses, for nearly half (44 percent) of the parents who had been raised in a fundamentalist faith no longer affiliated with a fundamentalist religion—one of the poorer retention records in the study. But the fundamentalists *did* win many converts, particularly from the Anglican, United, and Catholic Churches of Canada as they all became more "liberal." (See table 2 in Bob Altemeyer, "The Decline of Organized Religion in Western Civilization," in *International Journal for the Psychology of Religion* 14 [2004]: 77–89.) Whether the influx of converts will continue after the fundamentalists in other religions have found their way to the fundamentalist sects is anybody's guess. But if it does not, a 40+ percent loss rate per generation can only lead to one thing. At the same time, one must recognize that the sample is composed of parents of University of Manitoba students, and the fundamentalist churches may do better among those who do not send their children to a large public university.

6. Michael Hout and Claude S. Fischer, "Why More Americans Have No Religious Preference: Politics and Generations," *American Sociological Review* 67 (2002): 165–90.

7. Bob Altemeyer, "Changes in Attitudes toward Homosexuals," *Journal of Homosexuality* 42 (2001): 63–75.

8. Both studies are reported in Altemeyer, "The Decline of Organized Religion in Western Civilization," pp. 77–89. Ronald J. Sider, a professor at Eastern Baptist Theological Seminary, makes the point about hypocrisy among born-again and evangelical Christians very powerfully in chapter 1 of *The Scandal of the Evangelical Conscience* (Grand Rapids: Baker Books, 2005). He observed that, despite Jesus' unequivocal stand on the permanence of marriage, born-again and evangelical Christians divorce as often as others do. As their income has gone up, they have given a smaller and smaller percentage to charity. Despite Jesus' great concern for the poor, the public agenda of prominent evangelical political movements rarely includes justice for the poor. The number of unmarried couples living together jumped more in the Bible belt during the 1990s than in the nation as a whole. Of the evangelical youth who took a "True Love Waits" pledge to abstain from intercourse until marriage, 88 percent broke it. Baptists and evangelicals proved more likely to object to having black neighbors than any other religious group. And "saved" men are reportedly about as likely to use pornography, and to physically abuse their wives, as "unsaved" men.

9. In 1999, 364 University of Manitoba students were asked to answer a multiple-

choice test about the location of some famous Bible passages. Where, for example, would one find the passage, "In that region there were shepherds living in the fields, keeping watch over their flock by night . . . to you is born this day in the city of David a savior, who is the Messiah, the Lord"? Four possible answers were offered: Luke, Jeremiah, Psalms, and Genesis. As the last three are all from the Old Testament/Hebrew scriptures, the question should have been easy, but only 38 percent got it right—merely 13 percent above chance. The other three questions involved the much-advertised "For God so loved the world that he gave his only Son, so that everyone who believes in him may not perish but may have eternal life" (i.e., John 3:16); where one would find the story of Sampson and Delilah; and who said, "If I speak in the tongues of mortals and of angels, but do not have love . . . and the greatest of these is love." In all cases the alternatives offered should have made the question easy. Could one find the story of Sampson in Exodus or the Gospel of Matthew or (the most popular choice) the Acts of the Apostles (Sampson was an apostle of Jesus?)? But the mean percent correct over all four questions was 31.2, barely different from pure guessing's 25 percent. Religious fundamentalists (N = 88) did better on the quiz than most, but their overall score was still only 60 percent correct. They did best on that widely proclaimed John 3:16 (75 percent correct) and the Christmas story (69 percent), but failed the other questions, betraying a spotty knowledge of the book they say they hold above all others.

10. Altemeyer, "The Decline of Organized Religion in Western Civilization," pp. 77–89.

11. George Gallup Jr. and Frank Newport, "Religion in the Aftermath of September 11," in *Gallup Poll Monthly* (December 2001): 26–30.

12. According to Robert Todd Carroll in *The Skeptic's Dictionary* (Hoboken, NJ: Wiley, 2003), p. 39, "A world-wide survey in 2000 by the Gallup polling agency found that 8 percent do not think there is any spirit, personal God, or life force. Another 17 percent are not sure . . . more than half the world's population . . . do not believe in a personal God." So when someone says that every culture in the world believes in God, one might recall that different cultures can have radically different notions about what this supernatural force might be. Seemingly, those who believe in a personal God such as the Judeo-Christian deity are actually in a minority. And as we shall see, many Christians have different views of God than other Christians have.

CHAPTER 1

HOW WE STUDIED ATHEISTS

Welcome to the dullest but probably most important chapter in this book. People would naturally rather read about scientific discoveries than the methods used to make them. "Ends, si; Means, nyet!" The trouble is, in our business what you find very much depends on how you do your study. For example, "Is the president doing a good job?" People *usually* answer yes. But if you were to instead ask the same people, "Is the president doing a bad job?" a surprising number of those who would say yes to the first question would also say yes to the second. This is called "yea-saying." Many people, unless you really smack them with an objectionable notion like "The government should get all our money," agree with most ideas you present. Pollsters know about yea-saying, and so do savvy political staffs.[1]

So what you get depends, to a certain extent, not on what people actually think but on what question you ask. We believe we asked fair and square questions in our study of atheists—just being interested in the truth, no matter what it turned out to be. But you can decide for yourself if we did. And even with the best of intentions, we probably still made mistakes. That's also your call.

What you get also depends on *whom* you ask. We did not study run-of-the-mill American atheists—if 3 percent of the population can be called run-of-the-mill in any sense. Instead, we mainly studied persons who belonged to atheists clubs, and atheists clubs in the San Francisco Bay region to boot. If you think San Francisco oozes "liberalism" and so atheists from there might bear little resemblance to atheists elsewhere, we are on the same page. So we surveyed atheists clubs in Alabama and Idaho as well. Then we studied Canadian atheists (who did not belong to any atheists clubs), and to get a point of oppositeness, we investigated Canadians who scored very highly on a measure of religious fundamentalism.

All of which misses an ideal study by a country mile. Ideally, if you start off (as we did) with San Franciscan active atheists, you compare them with inactive, non-clubbing atheists in the same region. Then you survey some active, and inactive, highly religious folks with the same zip codes. Then you get the same four kinds of informants in other parts of the United States. Throw in some "normals" everywhere for luck while you are sampling far and wide. If you did all this, not only would you do the first broad study of atheists in America, you would probably do the all-time champion study of atheists anywhere.

We did not do anything so grand because we had neither the contacts nor the boodle to accomplish it. Accordingly, our samples could be both more diversified and better matched. We had to settle for doing the apparent first but certainly not the best possible study. But hooray for the scientific method, because if other researchers become interested in studying atheists, the problems will be addressed as our findings get tested elsewhere.

PROCEDURE: THE SAN FRANCISCO BAY AREA STUDY

Our study of atheists began when a member of the Atheists of Silicon Valley, Chris Lindstrom, asked in March of 2002 if we would be interested in surveying her group. She had just read our book *Amazing Conversions*, in which we presented two very different groups of university students. Some had had virtually no experience with religion as children, yet had become very religious. The other students had been steeped in their family religion, but then chucked it all. Chris thought her club had lots of the latter "amazing apostates," and invited us to study them. Furthermore, she said, other atheists clubs in the Bay Area might be interested. Chris thought we could get 150 responses, maybe more.

She did not have to ask twice. We said we would gladly do such a study, but we also added, "As you will appreciate, the study would have to be done in a way that would be scientifically beyond reproach, with no hint of biasing influence from the sponsoring organization." Chris wrote back, "I fully understand . . . that any study would most likely reveal some unflattering portraits as well as flattering ones. . . . [But] it's better to be (and be seen as) human beings." We then worked up an initial survey and sent it to Chris for suggestions about wording and anything we might have missed. "We're sure you understand that we can't tell you what the various surveys and questions measure, but I also imagine it will be pretty self-evident to anyone who reads the questions." Chris gave us a lot of useful feedback, particularly in wording our questions unambiguously for an atheist sample, and said six clubs had signed on for the survey.

We next worked out a procedure for getting the questionnaires to club members and then back to us, all the while guaranteeing anonymity. We would send Chris a bunch of packets. Each packet was enclosed in a University of Manitoba letter-sized envelope with a US 57¢ stamp on it. Chris, using a systematic rule such as "every third name on the mailing list," selected a sample of the membership of each club. The club member who received one of these envelopes found inside a letter of explanation from us printed on University of Manitoba letterhead (exhibit 1.1), a survey (which turned out to be seven pages long!), and another University of Manitoba envelope addressed to us, bearing a US 60¢ stamp. This procedure made it clear to the individual atheist that no one would know who participated in the study.

As we were paying for this study with dribs and drabs of funds from other research grants (please don't tell anyone), we at first intended to send out 200 surveys. But when the list of participating clubs rose to six, we upped our cast to 600. Chris distributed these among the organizations according to the size of their mailing lists, from the San Francisco Atheists to the Gay and Lesbian Atheists and Humanists (San Francisco chapter), including the East Bay Atheists, the Secular Humanists of the East Bay, the Humanist Community of Palo Alto, and the Atheists of Silicon Valley. After busily sticking stamps and packing packets in the high school library in Pembina, North Dakota, on May 10, we shipped the lot off to Chris. She received them on the fifteenth, and soon they were zipping through the mail system around San Francisco Bay. We got the first returns on the twenty-fourth, and they continued to arrive throughout the summer, eventually totaling 304—a good return rate for an "out of the blue, from nobody you ever heard of " mail-back survey about personal beliefs. However, one came back chopped into little pieces, so maybe we should say we received replies from only 303. And eight others had to be discarded because the respondent opted not to answer a lot of the questions. Still others said they were agnostics, not atheists, so we dropped them from the study, too. At the end we had 253 usable surveys from atheists who belonged to atheists clubs in the San Francisco area.

We shall be describing each of the surveys in our booklet in the following chapters, but you can see the whole Bay Area questionnaire in the appendix. In overview, we first established whether the respondent really was an atheist. Then we made a number of inquiries about the individual's religious background. After that, we asked some open-ended questions designed to trace the person's religious journey. What had made him an atheist? Then we got into some heavy-duty measures of dogmatism, zealotry, and religious prejudice. We finished up with some demographic questions.

Speaking of demographics, recall our question from the introduction, "Who are those guys?" Some of them happened not to be guys at all, but 69 percent of the 253 responding atheists were. Their median age of sixty[2] made them as time-honored and antediluvian as the authors of this book—which implies that these atheists clubs may soon have the same problem many symphony orchestras do as their audiences grow old, die, and definitely do not renew. They had gone to school a lot, especially for their generation, putting in a median seventeen years of formal education. Most (57 percent) were married. Politically, 60 percent said they usually voted Democratic and only 3 percent supported Republicans. (The rest were Independents, "Greens," "Others," or "Nones.")

Exhibit 1.1
Letter Sent to the San Francisco Bay Area Atheists

May 8, 2002

Dear Friend:

I and my colleague Bruce Hunsberger are professors of psychology in Canada who have been studying religious beliefs and attitudes for many years. As you can probably imagine, most of our samples have been dominated by persons who believe in the traditional Judeo-Christian God. Virtually no studies have been done of atheists or agnostics. We are trying to redress this imbalance now.

An atheists club to which you belong has cooperated in this endeavor by forwarding the envelope you just opened. We have been provided with no membership list, and have no idea who is receiving our letters. Furthermore, the fact that your club forwarded this letter for us does not mean you are *in any way* obliged to participate in this study. We would only want you to participate if you freely chose to do so. But if you serve, you will be anonymous. Neither we, nor any one else, will ever know who decided to participate, and who decided not to. *All participants will be completely anonymous.*

Our survey begins on the *back side of this piece of paper*. We invite you to look it over, to see what we are asking, to get an idea of what the study is trying to discover. We believe everything is quite obvious. It will probably take you 30 minutes to an hour to answer the survey. Of course, you can skip any part of it that you wish, but we hope you will respond to all we ask. If we have not given you enough room to answer some questions, please feel free to write in the margins or on extra pieces of paper. If you have questions about anything, you can email me at <altemey@cc.umanitoba.ca>.

Once you have completed the survey, would you please put it in the enclosed envelope and send it back to me. It would be especially helpful if you could do this sometime in the next week. Then, after we have tabulated the responses, we shall send a full *statistical summary* of the results to your atheists club, and ask it to make the findings available at the next meeting.

If you have taken courses in the behavioral sciences, you may know there is a particular danger to the validity of a study done this way. When participants know they have been contacted because they are members of some particular organization, they sometimes answer the way they think "members of our club" *should* answer. We don't want that. We want *your* answers, whether you think they are representative of your club or not.

Finally, persons who agree to serve in a study like this are usually asked to sign an informed consent sheet, proving they were told what the study involved and they freely agreed to participate. However, signing such a form would make it impossible for you to serve anonymously. So, whoever you are, we shall do the obvious and assume that *if* you fill out our survey, you have read this letter, looked over the questionnaire, and freely agreed to participate. (If you don't, we won't be hearing from you, will we?) This research project has been approved by the Psychology/Sociology Research Ethics Board of the University of Manitoba. Any complaints can be directed to the Board at 204-474-7122.

Please see the other side of this page if you wish to have your answers be part of this study.

Sincerely,
Robert A. Altemeyer, Ph.D.

PROCEDURE: THE ALABAMA AND IDAHO ATHEISTS CLUBS

By July 2002 we knew what the Bay Area survey was turning up, and immediately wondered if one would find the same things in other American atheists clubs. Working from the Web site of the American Atheists, we e-mailed solicitations to twenty-one local chapters asking if we could also study their members? Only three groups responded, all with very small memberships: the Mobile, Alabama, Atheists (N = 15), the Birmingham, Alabama, Atheists (N = 10), and the Idaho Atheists (N = 25). We mailed each club enough packets for its entire membership on August 26, and by the end of September (when we told the Bay Area clubs what we had found in studying them) we had heard from eleven, nine, and fifteen of the respective clubs' members.[3] But seven of these thirty-five were agnostics, so our tiny cross-validating sample got whittled down to just twenty-eight atheists. Demographically, these twenty-eight proved a little less dominated by Y-chromosomes than the Bay Area atheists had been (62 percent versus 69 percent), they had not lived as long (56.5 years on the average compared with 60), nor had they gone to school as much (sixteen years versus seventeen). We probed into marital backgrounds and found 42 percent were currently married, 23 percent were divorced, 19 percent were widowed, and 12 percent were not married but had long-term partners. Politically, 46 percent favored the Democrats, 3 percent the Republicans, and the rest were Independents, "Others," or "Nones."

How do all these numbers compare with what we can glean about American atheists in general from the national polls? Well, the total of thirty-three persons in the 2000 General Social Survey[4] who said they did not believe that God exists were two-thirds male (which lands close to our San Francisco and Alabama/Idaho compositions), but they were substantially younger on the average (41.7 years) and less educated (14.0 years). So we can say from the get-go that our *active* American atheist respondents do not represent American atheists in general—which we suspected from the get-go. But of course active American atheists seem very much worth studying in their own right.

PROCEDURE: THE MANITOBA PARENT STUDY

Once we had a whiff of the Bay Area results, we attempted to administer a "theist" version of our questionnaire to very religious persons—ideally from the same geographic region. But we could not establish California contacts. In the end the best we could do was devote an annual survey of Manitoba parents to the issues we raised in our study of American atheists, ultimately comparing atheist parents with very religious ones.

Most years, for several decades, hundreds of introductory psychology students at the University of Manitoba have been involved in survey research that mainly deals with right-wing authoritarianism. As well, their parents have sometimes been invited to answer a booklet that earns their children a small part of the intro psych grade. Perhaps because their own genes are usually at stake, parents have shown a remarkable willingness to fill out long booklets of surveys for such minor and indirect rewards.

In the fall of 2002, 475 students took home a packet containing a solicitous letter (see exhibit 1.2), a survey booklet, and two optical-scan "bubble sheets" for their parents' responses.[5] Of these, 418 pairs of response sheets came back (almost always from the mother and father, but occasionally from a mother and aunt, etc.). One of the questions answered by the 836 parents asked if the parent believed in the traditional God (a thinking being who created the universe, was almighty and eternal, all-loving and all-good, constantly aware of our lives, who hears our prayers, and will judge us after we die). Three possible answers were provided:

> I am an **atheist**. I do not believe in the existence of this "traditional" God. I believe it does *not* exist.
>
> I am an **agnostic**. I do not believe in the existence of this "traditional" God, *nor* do I disbelieve in it.[6]
>
> I am a **theist**. I believe in the existence of this "traditional" God.

Fifty-one (6 percent) of the 836 parents said they were atheists. Males appeared slightly less often (61 percent) than they had among our active American atheists, the parent atheists were rather younger (forty-eight years on the average), and they had less education (fifteen years).[7] They were spread all over the Canadian political map.

How did we identify "very religious parents"? The survey booklet began with a Religious Fundamentalism scale that measures the belief that there is one set of religious teachings that clearly contains the fundamental, basic, intrinsic, essential, inerrant truth about humanity and deity. The scale also taps the belief that Satan exists and fights this fundamental truth, that the truth must be followed today according to the practices of the past, and those who follow this truth have a special relationship with God.[8] Half the sample answered the original twenty-item version of the scale and the rest responded to the updated twelve-item version shown in exhibit 1.3. Why don't you answer the updated version now to get a feel for the sentiments involved?

Each answer on the -4 to +4 system is converted onto a 1 to 9 scale. For half the items, such as no. 1, +4 gets a 9. But for the others, such as no. 2, the staunch fundamentalist says -4. (This controls for that yea-saying mentioned at the beginning of this chapter. If you answer +4 to everything, you will land in the exact middle of the possible scores.) We selected the twenty-six parents with the highest scores on this twelve-item version, and the twenty-five in the other half of the sample who similarly topped the distribution of the twenty-item scores, to compose a group of believers that was as decidedly religious as the fifty-one parent atheists were decidedly nonreligious.[9] The resulting forty-seven Christian and four Muslim "High Fun-

Exhibit 1.2
Letter Sent to Manitoba Parents

October 8, 2002

Dear Parent:

I am a professor of psychology at the University of Manitoba, where your daughter/son is taking introductory psychology this year. As you may know, it is possible for students in this course to earn a small part of their grade by serving as subjects in studies being conducted by members of my department. This enables the students to learn about psychological research firsthand, and also helps us do the research on which the science of psychology is based.

One problem with this system is that most of our research tends to be done with university students, instead of with other persons who might be more typical of the population as a whole. So I am interested in collecting survey data from parents of university students, to do a more general study of social attitudes.

Your child indicated, by forwarding this material to you, that s/he thought you would not mind completing the booklet enclosed. If you do so, and get the answer sheet back to me by **October 31,** 2002, I'll be able to give your child three experimental credits for helping me collect the data.

Having said all this, let me also say I want to keep you from feeling "pressured" by me or by anyone else to complete the booklet. The experimental credits involved are worth only a tiny part of the grade in Introductory Psychology, and there are many other ways students can earn these credits. *Furthermore, this is a long booklet and will probably take you about an hour and a half to complete.* There is absolutely **no** penalty to students whose parents decline to participate. So please only complete the survey if you are genuinely willing to do so.

I shall give a general summary of the results of this study to students in March. You will be able to find out about these results then by asking your daughter/son.

You will note there is no place for you to sign your name on the survey. It is to be answered ANONYMOUSLY. *All you should return to me* is the "bubble sheet" enclosed in the booklet.

If you decide to participate, please use a **pencil** to mark your answers on the "bubble sheet." And please answer *on your own.* That is, do not consult beforehand with your spouse, child, etc. It is essential for the scientific value of the study that the responses come from you as an individual, answering alone.

Finally, persons who agree to serve in a study like this are usually asked to sign an informed consent sheet, proving they were told what the study involved and they freely agreed to participate. However, signing such a form would make it impossible for you to serve anonymously. So we shall do the obvious and assume that *if* you fill out our survey, you have freely agreed to participate. This research project has been approved by the Psychology/Sociology Research Ethics Board of the University of Manitoba. Any complaints can be directed to Dr. Bruce Tefft, Chair of the Board, at 204-474-8259. If you have any questions about this project, please call me at 204-474-9276 or email me at "altemey@cc.umanitoba.ca."

Sincerely,
Robert A. Altemeyer, Ph.D.

Exhibit 1.3
The 12-Item Religious Fundamentalism Scale

This survey is part of an investigation of general public opinion concerning a variety of social issues. You will probably find that you *agree* with some of the statements, and *disagree* with others, to varying extents. Please indicate your reaction to each statement according to the following scale:

Write down a -4 if you *very strongly disagree* with the statement.

-3 if you *strongly disagree* with the statement.

-2 if you *moderately disagree* with the statement.

-1 if you *slightly disagree* with the statement.

Write down a +1 if you *slightly agree* with the statement.

+2 if you *moderately agree* with the statement.

+3 if you *strongly agree* with the statement.

+4 if you *very strongly agree* with the statement.

If you feel exactly and precisely *neutral* about an item, blacken the "0" bubble.

You may find that you sometimes have different reactions to different parts of a statement. For example, you might very strongly disagree ("-4") with one idea in a statement, but slightly agree ("+1") with another idea in the same item. When this happens, please combine your reactions, and write down how you feel on balance (a "-3" in this case).

___ 1. God has given humanity a complete, unfailing guide to happiness and salvation, which must be totally followed.

___ 2. No single book of religious teachings contains all the intrinsic, fundamental truths about life.

___ 3. The basic cause of evil in this world is Satan, who is still constantly and ferociously fighting against God.

___ 4. It is more important to be a good person than to believe in God and the right religion.

___ 5. There is a particular set of religious teachings in this world that are so true, you can't go any "deeper" because they are the basic, bedrock message that God has given humanity.

___ 6. When you get right down to it, there are basically only two kinds of people in the world: the Righteous, who will be rewarded by God; and the rest, who will not.

___ 7. Scriptures may contain general truths, but they should NOT be considered completely, literally true from beginning to end.

___ 8. To lead the best, most meaningful life, one must belong to the one, fundamentally true religion.

___ 9. "Satan" is just the name people give to their own bad impulses. There really is *no such thing* as a diabolical "Prince of Darkness" who tempts us.

___ 10. Whenever science and sacred scripture conflict, *science* is probably right.

___ 11. The fundamentals of God's religion should never be tampered with, or compromised with others' beliefs.

___ 12. *All* of the religions in the world have flaws and wrong teachings. There is *no* perfectly true, right religion.

Note: Responses are scored as follows. For Items 1, 3, 5, 6, 8 and 11, a -4 is coded as 1, a -3 is coded as 2, a -2 is coded as 3, a -1 is coded as 4, a 0 is coded as 5, a +1 is coded as 6, a +2 is coded as 7, a +3 is coded as 8, and a +4 is coded as 9. For the other items, the scoring key is reversed. That is, for Item 2 a -4 is coded as 9, -3 is coded as 8, and so on up to +4 being coded as 1. One's score on the Religious Fundamentalism scale is the sum of the 12 item scores.

damentalists" tended to be female (51 percent) by the narrowest of margins, and forty-eight years old with thirteen years of formal education on the average. Politically they supported Canada's right-wing Alliance (20 percent) and Reform (16 percent) parties more than most parents did.

How do these highly fundamentalist Manitoba parents compare with ordinary fundamentalists in America? The best answer is provided by an outstanding doctoral dissertation produced by T. Witzig in 2005.[10] Witzig sent survey packets to 1,016 randomly selected members of an unnamed fundamentalist Protestant denomination. The names and addresses were obtained from church directories, and members were surveyed throughout the United States. The booklet was long and some of the surveys dealt with personal adjustment issues, so you might expect a miniscule return rate. But because the denomination cooperated in the study, and because Witzig offered each person a free CD of hymns for serving in his study, he got back 302 usable questionnaires. His sample was 60 percent female, 49.1 years old on the average, and had a mean 13.7 years of education. Eighty-six percent had been raised in the denomination involved.

Witzig included the original twenty-item version of the Religious Fundamentalism scale in his booklet, and his 302 respondents produced the highest sample mean we have ever seen on the instrument: 141.2. The highest-scoring group in our own studies, Manitoba parents affiliated with fundamentalist Protestant denominations, average around 130. One cannot say how representative Witzig's sample is of America's "religious right"—but it might not surprise many Canadians if American fundamentalists turn out to be more fundamentalist than their Canadian counterparts.

But the Manitoba parents we split off for comparison with the atheist parents scored even higher on the Religious Fundamentalism scale, posting a mean of 153.8 on the twenty-item version (see note 9). They comprise an artificial group, not members of any one church but simply individuals who had very fundamentalist views about whatever religion they belonged to. Will their results transfer to the American scene? Will American fundamentalists tend to behave the way this artificial group did in our study? The *one* comparison available, Witzig's, indicates our High Fundamentalist Manitoba parent sample is basically comparable to the average member of an American Protestant fundamentalist denomination, but it also is slightly (153.8/141.2 = 1.09) more religiously fundamentalist.

SUMMARY

We asked various groups of people to anonymously answer a long questionnaire about their religious beliefs. Most of the people in all of these groups kindly did so. We ended up with a large sample of active atheists from the San Francisco Bay Area, and another sample of active atheists, one-tenth the San Francisco size, from Alabama and Idaho. Neither group represents American atheists as a whole, but they probably offer a reasonably good look at the active atheists who launch lawsuits against school prayer, the teaching of creation science, and so on. We also have data from atheist parents of Canadian university students. They differ so much from the active American atheists (e.g., in nationality, age, involvement with atheism as a movement, and average temperature endured during winter) that comparing them with the Americans would not constitute "apples with oranges," but be more like "apples with strawberries," or maybe "frozen strawberries." Finally, we have some other Canadian parents who scored very high on a measure of religious fundamentalism ("anti-strawberries"?). They appear comparable to the average American fundamentalist, if modestly "more so." But more importantly, these fifty-one Manitoba high fundamentalists can be compared with the fifty-one Manitoba atheists from the same study, letting us see how different strong theists are from atheists. *And* how similar they may be.

NOTES

1. Why do people yea-say? Well, not everyone does. Both of our wives, for example, tend to nay-say instead. But in general people learn early in life that the "right" response when a parent, teacher, scout leader, and so on says something is usually to agree. Some people never outgrow this; persons with an authoritarian personality, who are more inclined to submit to established authority than most, tend to yea-say a lot. (See Bob Altemeyer, *The Authoritarian Specter* [Cambridge, MA: Harvard University Press, 1996], pp. 62–63.) Yea-saying probably occurs most in polls when the respondent wants to please the pollster, does not understand the question, or has little interest in giving accurate answers.

2. We usually report "averages" in terms of the median, which is the score in the exact center of the distribution. We believe this gives a fairer picture of what the average person in the group is like than the usual scientific measure, called the mean, which can be swished around quite a bit by unusually high or unusually low scores. Medians, however, cannot be used in the powerful statistical tests of significance that researchers live and die by. We shall present the means of interesting scores in the endnotes (for example, see n. 7 below) for those who care, where they won't be such speed bumps in our narrative.

3. The Alabama-Idaho booklet ran to only five pages, as we dropped several surveys from the Bay Area questionnaire that had produced little variability. We also reworded some of our open-ended questions to make them clearer. The changes will be noted in the following chapters. The shorter survey may have led to the higher response rates.

4. We cite the 2000 GSS survey because the question about belief in God was not asked in 2002 or 2004.

5. As will be seen, we had "believer" and "nonbeliever" versions of some of our measures, so we had to make up two different sets of booklets. A traditional approach would have been to send these out randomly among the parents, but that would mean a lot of useless data from, for example, believers answering questions designed to measure things about atheists. So we tried to make an informed guess of which booklet to send to each household by asking the students to indicate on their (preceding) questionnaire, "How religious would you say your mother (and then father) is in terms of her beliefs?" The students answered on a linear scale identified at various points as "Not at all," "Slightly," "Moderately," "Strongly," and "Very Strongly." We sent the atheist version of the booklet to homes where at least one parent

was reported to be "Not at all" to "Slightly" religious. And we sent the "believer" version to homes where at least one parent was reported "Strongly" to "Very Strongly" in beliefs. (A few homes, no doubt interesting ones, had both kinds of parents and we sent them the atheist or believer version at random, as we did for the many homes that had neither an atheist nor a strong believer.) It turned out that sometimes the kids did not know how religious their parents were—especially when the parents were not very religious. But this procedure did enable us to get the atheist version of the booklet into the hands of a solid majority (38) of the 51 parents who turned out to be atheists, and the believer version to nearly all (45) of the 51 strong believers.

6. Agnosticism is often defined in dictionaries as the belief that one cannot *ever* know whether God exists. We have taken a softer line, defining agnosticism as uncertainty on the matter, but with no stand on what the future might bring. We shall present the Manitoba agnostics' responses to the booklet in chapter 9.

7. The *mean* age of the Manitoba parent atheists was 47.7 with a standard deviation of 6.8, and their mean level of education equaled 15.2 years with an "sd" of 3.6. The figures for the Manitoba parent high fundamentalists were 47.8 (6.7) and 13.7 (3.6). The Bay Area atheists' mean age equaled 58.5 years, with a standard deviation of 15.8. Level of education in this sample had a mean of 17.5 years (3.2). The corresponding values for the Alabama/Idaho atheists were 56.5 (17.6) and 16.8 (3.7).

8. This model of religious fundamentalism, and the original twenty-item "RF" scale, was first presented by Bob Altemeyer and Bruce Hunsberger in "Authoritarianism, Religious Fundamentalism, Quest, and Prejudice," *International Journal for the Psychology of Religion* 2 (1992): 113–33. The twelve-item version shown in exhibit 2.3 was presented in that same journal in 2004, pp. 47–54, in a paper titled, "A Revised Religious Fundamentalism Scale: The Short and Sweet of It."

9. Why did we use two versions of the RF scale? We were testing the revised, shortened form against the original version. The mean score on the twenty-item scale answered by 412 parents was a nonfundamental 76.7 (sd = 33.3). The mean of the 190 inter-item correlations within the test equaled 0.38, producing an alpha reliability coefficient of 0.93 for the measure as a whole. The results for the 424 sets of responses to the twelve-item RF scale were as follows: sample mean = 50.8 (28.5), mean inter-item correlation = 0.49; alpha = 0.92. "High Fundamentalists" scored between 140 and 179 on the twenty-item scale (N = 25), and between 98 and 108 on the twelve-item version (N = 26) shown in exhibit 2.3.

10. Theodore F. Witzig Jr., "Obsessional Beliefs, Religious Beliefs, and Scrupulosity among Fundamental Protestant Christians," *Dissertation Abstracts International*, § B: The Sciences & Engineering, vol. 65 (7-B), 3735 (University Microfilms International, 2005).

CHAPTER 2

ARE THE "ATHEISTS" REALLY ATHEISTS?

"I Believe in God, the Father Almighty . . ."

B efore we start analyzing people as atheists, hadn't we better make sure they really are? Accordingly, this brief chapter will look at how our various samples responded to questions about the traditional God, whether they believe any sort of supernatural force works in the universe, and how much they doubt the value of religion and religious practices.

What precisely is an atheist? In *Atheism*, philosopher George Smith (1989) defines it as "the absence of theistic belief" (p. 3). This does not necessarily entail *dis*belief. But most dictionaries make the distinction, typically defining an atheist as one who *denies* the existence of God, an agnostic as one who holds that the existence of God is unknown, and a theist as one who believes God exists. If we can semantically concur on that much, can we agree on what this "God" might be? Is it presently alive or dead? All-powerful or limited? Constantly attentive and loving, or profoundly indifferent?

We began our survey of the Bay Area atheists by asking them about seven traditional attributes of the Judeo-Christian God.

One of the 253 respondents did not answer the first question, about a thinking, self-aware God; the other 252 said no.[1] Ninety-nine percent said no to the question about an *almighty* God, 98 percent said they did not believe in a God that created the universe for its own purposes, and 100 percent said they did not believe in a God that is aware of us and hears our prayers, that is all-loving and good, and that will judge us after death. To put it another way, of the (253 × 7 =) 1,771 possible responses in this sample, 5 were "No Responses," 8 were "Yes," and 1,758 were "No." In other words, "No way, St. Thomas A."

Because of the overwhelming consistency of these responses, we did not ask these questions again in the shortened survey sent to the Alabama and Idaho clubs. However, the answers given by the 51 Manitoba parent atheists strongly resembled

---

A. *People have different concepts of "God." Do you believe in a supernatural power, a deity:*

That is a thinking, self-aware being, not just some
physical force like the "Big Bang"?   ___ No ___ Yes

That is almighty, can do anything it decides to do?   ___ No ___ Yes

That is eternal: always was, and always will be?   ___ No ___ Yes

That intentionally created the universe for its own purposes?   ___ No ___ Yes

That is constantly aware of our individual lives and
hears our prayers?   ___ No ___ Yes

That is all-loving and all-good?   ___ No ___ Yes

That will judge us after we die, sending some to Heaven
and others to Hell?   ___ No ___ Yes

---

those obtained from the Bay Area: of the (51 × 7 =) 357 responses given, 5 were "Yes" and the other 352 were "No." In contrast, the 51 *highly fundamentalist* parents answered with 349 "Yes's" and only 8 "No's." So, to conclude the obvious and predictable, the self-declared atheists clearly do NOT believe in the traditional Judeo-Christian God, and the strong fundamentalists very definitely say they do.[2]

We then asked the samples to choose among the self-labels of "atheist," "agnostic," and "theist," to which all the atheists in our study answered, "atheist," and all the fundamentalists, "theists." We also asked the Americans: "What name/term do you personally prefer to use to describe yourself (e.g., humanist, atheist, non-believer, un-believer, non-theist, heretic)?" Most Bay Area respondents preferred "atheist," but about one-third called themselves "humanists." The Alabama/Idaho samples responded similarly, with 71 percent saying they preferred "atheist," and most of the remainder preferring "humanist."

Pushing the issue of a supernatural power further, we inquired among the Bay Area sample:

C. *If you do not believe in the "traditional" God,* is there any sense in which you do believe in "God"? *If so, would you please describe what kind of God or supernatural being or supernatural force that you DO believe in? Does this being play an active role in human lives? (If so, how?)*

Only 15 (6 percent) of the 253 atheists said they believed in *any* kind of supernatural power, and their names for it (e.g., "Nature," "Life Force," "Laws of the Universe") imply even these are not *super*natural entities.

In conclusion, the atheist samples appear to be deep-down, hard-core, all the way to their socks, "I mean it when I say it" atheists. They deny the existence of any sort of divine being.

RELIGIOUS DOUBTS

If you would like yet more detailed information about what our atheists do not believe, all our samples answered a twenty-item Religious Doubts scale, shown in exhibit 2.1. Why don't you answer it yourself now, so you can get a feel for the issues it raises. For each item, simply write down the extent to which *you presently have doubts about religion, serious concerns about the basic truth of religion,* because of that factor. Just ignore the numbers after each item, and put down *your* answer, using the following response scale:

   0 = To no extent at all
   1 = To a slight extent
   2 = To a mild extent
   3 = To a moderate extent
   4 = To an appreciable extent
   5 = To a considerable extent
   6 = To a great extent

When you have finished, add up your answers. If you had no doubts whatsoever, your total score would be a minimalist 0 (and you would be a very rare respondent). If you have max-ed out doubts on all the issues, you would hit $(20 \times 6 =)$ 120, the highest total possible—also rare. The midpoint of possible scores equals 60. Parents of students at the University of Manitoba average 40-something—indicating a "mild" level of doubt overall. How do you compare with these middle-class, middle-aged, middle-country Canadians?

Now let's look at those numbers after each item. You first see two numbers in parentheses—e.g., (6; 6) after item 1. Those show the median—i.e., again, the middle score in the distribution of answers to that item—in the Bay Area and the Alabama/Idaho samples respectively. The sixes mean (ta dum!) that these active atheists hugely doubted the existence of God. Then we come to a number in square brackets—e.g., [5]. That shows the median for the 51 Manitoba parent atheists, which means their average guy doubted the existence of God "to a considerable extent." (Yes, the fact that these atheists did not also rack up a six on this item strikes one as a little goofy, but that's the way the numbers crunched.) Last comes the {0}, which is the median for the 51 Manitoba parent fundamentalists, showing they had no doubt at all about God's existence. No surprise there, huh?

Exhibit 2.1
The Religious Doubts Scale

_____ 1. The existence of God, an all-good, all-powerful
supreme being who created the universe.   (6; 6) [5] {0}

_____ 2. The problem of evil and unfair suffering in the
world.   (5; 5) [4] {1}

_____ 3. The history of religion; bad things religions did
in the past.   (5; 5.5) [5] {1}

_____ 4. Evolution vs. Creation.   (6; 6) [4] {0}

_____ 5. The way religious people sometimes pressured
others to believe what they believe.   (4; 5)[4] {1}

_____ 6. The hypocrisy of "religious" people (i.e., the
nonreligious behaviour of supposedly religious people). (4; 5) [5] {1}

_____ 7. Getting to know people from other religions, or
people with no religion.   (3; 3) [2] {0}

_____ 8. The death of a loved one.   (0; 0) [1] {1}

_____ 9. Religious teachings about sex.   (2; 2.5) [2] {0}

_____ 10. The way some religious people seemed interested
mainly in getting money from others.   (3; 4) [3] {1}

_____ 11. The intolerance some religious people showed
toward other religions.   (4; 6) [5] {1}

_____ 12. Religious teachings about the role of women.   (4; 4.5) [3] {1}

_____ 13. Threats about what would happen if you were bad
(e.g., being condemned to hell).   (3; 4) [3] {0}

_____ 14. Finding that being religious did not bring peace
and joy after all.   (2; 4.5) [2] {0}

_____ 15. The intolerance some religious people showed
toward certain other people (e.g., homosexuals).   (4; 5) [5] {0}

_____ 16. Claims that the Bible is the word of God.   (5; 5) [5] {0}

_____ 17. The way religion kept people from enjoying
themselves in sensible ways.   (3; 4.5) [3] {0}

_____ 18. Religious teachings often did not make sense;
they seemed contradictory, or unbelievable.   (6; 6) [5] {0}

_____ 19. What happens to us when we die? Is there really
an afterlife?   (5; 5) [4] {0}

_____ 20. Religious faith made people "blind," not questioning
teachings that should be questioned.   (5; 6) [5] {0}

Doubts

Let's get some overall impressions first. The total doubt score for the Bay Area atheists averaged 74, and the middle person in the Alabama/Idaho lineup banged out an 81.5. (The fourteenth atheist in the twenty-eight-person group got an 81 and the fifteenth rang up an 82.) These scores beat hollow the previous record for Religious Doubts scores, but the Manitoba parent atheists placed right with them, averaging 73. Manitoba parent fundamentalists, as you would expect, barely tipped the scale at 18 (less than "slight doubt").[3]

So what? Well, most of the atheists in our study belong to San Francisco atheists clubs. Because that is a reputedly godless corner of the continent, and these people are seemingly active in the cause of atheism, we should be asking (as we said in chapter 1), "How *un*representative is this main sample?" The overall data from the Religious Doubts scale provide some reassurance, as far as active atheists go at least. Our 253 informants from wild and woolly San Francisco might be wildly doubtful about religion compared with ordinary American atheists, but they actually posted lower scores than the Alabama/Idaho contingent. So the Bay Area sample is not unusually unusual *for active American atheists*—at least on this point. They do not even appear unusual compared with our tame but woolly Manitoba atheists—but that is a comparison fraught with complications.

Let us then look at the averages for each item, especially those in the first set of parentheses. What did NOT cause doubt in these respondents' minds? Death (item 8) did not—which strikes one because most of the Bay Area atheists, median age equal 60, have probably lost their parents, lots of friends, some spouses, and perhaps some of their children. Some people find it harder to believe in a good God after a loved one dies, especially if the death was painful or tragic. But the active American atheists say such losses, such depression, such anger, such fear of their own deaths, did not themselves lead them to doubt religion.

Neither did religious teachings about sex (item 9). Some may suspect that atheists reject religion because they want to wallow in wantonness. Nonbelievers may be perceived as licentious, their lust leading them away from God into the arms of "that old Satan." But the atheists did not particularly fault religious teachings about sex. Nor did they thunder in resentment at "the way religion kept people from enjoying themselves in sensible ways" (item 17).

Nor did the Bay Area atheists and the Manitoba atheists reject religion because it failed to bring them peace and joy (item 14). Peace and joy were not the issues for them.

Then what did produce doubt, if it was not anger, fear, lust, resentment, and emotional letdowns? Mainly things more cerebral. God could not be shown to exist (item 1). Accounts of creation did not square with the evidence supporting evolution (item 4). The Bible hardly seems to be the word of God (item 16). Teachings did not make sense (item 18). How could one know if there really is an afterlife (item 19)? And religion discouraged inquiry (item 20). To be sure, various failures of religion also played a large role, such as the inability to explain the evil and suffering in the world, the bad things religion did in the past, the hypocrisy of "religious people," and intolerance toward other religions and homosexuals. But what's really "the matter" with these people? The matters that weighed heaviest, and piled up the biggest numbers on the Doubts scale, involved ideas. Did religious teachings make sense? Did they correspond with scientific evidence? Could they stand up to examination and criticism? Religion, for these people, failed these tests.

For all of that, let us notice one last thing before moving on to the question of how (not why) the atheists became atheists. The median Doubt scores for our samples of active atheists ran from 74 to 81.5. But the Doubts scale itself runs all the way to 120. Here we are, looking at some of the most unreligious Americans you could possibly find, who posted the highest Doubts scores ever seen. But even so, they fell way short of maxing out. In fact they ended up closer to the midpoint on the scale (60) than the high end. That undoubtedly speaks to the care with which they answered the survey. They could have just written "6" to everything to dramatize their disbelief. Instead they appear to have responded to each item according to its personal relevance, and if their answer was zero, that's what they said. But it may also speak to the way religion can permeate a society. One *could,* rightly or wrongly, doubt the basic truth of religion for all of the twenty reasons given in exhibit 2.1. But it appears very few take it that far, even among the ranks of active atheists.

NOTES

1. Throughout this book we shall follow the convention of ignoring "no responses" when calculating percentages. That is, they shall be dropped from the denominator, and the percentage given will be what statistical packages usually call the "valid percent." Obviously this can be misleading when a lot of NRs occur. But that seldom happened in these studies. For example, among the seven questions about the attributes of God, the largest number of NR's for any question equaled 3 out of 253.

2. At least, that is their usual response, even when answering privately and anonymously. However, as we shall see in chapter 7, it turns out that, when asked in very special circumstances involving a "Hidden Observer," about a third of highly religious students admit that they have secret doubts that no one knows about concerning the existence of the traditional God. See Bob Altemeyer, *Enemies of Freedom* (San Francisco: Jossey-Bass, 1987), pp. 151–54.

3. Here are the means and standard deviations of the Religious Doubts scores for the four groups: San Francisco Atheists: 71.6 (27.1); Alabama/Idaho Atheists: 82.1 (22.8); Manitoba parent atheists: 70.0 (23.3); and Manitoba parent fundamentalists: 21.3 (17.1). If you wonder about statistical significance, all three atheist means are (obviously) significantly higher than the fundamentalist mean. Among the atheists, the Alabama/Idaho mean is significantly higher ($t = 2.06$; $p < 0.05$) than the Bay Area mean. If you care about the internal consistency of responses to the Religious Doubts scales, the mean of the inter-item correlations among the Bay Area atheists equaled 0.38, 0.35 among the Alabama/Idaho group, and 0.38 among the Manitoba parents. These figures led to alpha reliabilities of 0.92, 0.91, and 0.92 respectively.

CHAPTER 3

HOW DO PEOPLE
BECOME ATHEISTS?

W here do atheists come from? Well, where do theists come from? If you think the answer to the second question is, "It's mainly because of religious training during their youth," pat yourself on the back because research shows the best predictor of people's religiosity, so far at least, is how much religion was emphasized to them as they grew up.[1] So maybe atheists simply come from *non*religious backgrounds.

Time to get out your pencil again to answer another of the measures we used in our American studies. *To what extent did you have a "religious upbringing"?* That is, to what extent, adding it all up, did the important people in your life—such as your parents, teachers, and church officials (if any)—do the things listed in exhibit 3.1 as you were growing up?

0 = To no extent at all
1 = To a slight extent
2 = To a mild extent
3 = To a moderate extent
4 = To an appreciable extent
5 = To a considerable extent
6 = To a great extent

When you have finished, add up your twenty answers. If you had no religious upbringing whatsoever, your total score would smack rock bottom at 0. If you were thoroughly steeped in the family religion in every way mentioned, you would max out at 120. The middle of the possible scores, just as with the Doubts scale, equals 60. The average score of Manitoba parents currently hovers around 40, less than "moderate" and probably much lower than American norms.

The San Francisco atheists averaged 20.0—"to a slight extent" overall. The Alabama/Idaho sample came in significantly higher at 41.5—closer to ordinary, but probably still lower than most Americans. Figure 3.1 shows how the Religious Emphasis scores spread out across the possible range of results. You can immediately see that *most* of these atheists had little or no religious training during childhood, especially those in the San Francisco sample, confirming our obvious hunch about the roots of their atheism.[2] Why was so little emphasis placed on religion in a country so relatively religious? About 30 percent of the sample had at least one atheistic or agnostic parent, and many other future atheists came from parents who apparently believed in God but otherwise had little interest in religion. "Stony soil" indeed for nurturing faith.

But what about the atheists who came from religious backgrounds? Nearly a quarter had scores over 60 ("To a moderate extent") and over 10 percent had scores over 80 ("To an appreciable extent"). These "amazing atheists" *dis*confirm our obvious hunch because somehow they went against their rather strong religious training and cast it all aside. They did not simply stop going to church and become "lapsed Catholics" and "inactive Protestants" or "cultural Jews." They dropped all their religious beliefs, starting with "I believe in God . . ." How on earth could their socialization fail so completely? Don't psychologists believe child rearing determines everything else?

Maybe their socialization did not fail, but instead worked too well. In 1994–1995 we surveyed over four thousand Canadian university students, and identified those very few (fifty-eight) who had come from strong religious backgrounds, but had since dropped the family religion. We managed to interview most (forty-six) of these "Amazing Apostates," searching for the reasons behind their dramatic change.[3] More than anything else, they said they gave up their faith because they could not make themselves believe what they had been taught. Often they indicated they truly wished they could believe. Often they had paid a huge price in terms of ruptured family ties and lost friends for giving up their religion. Often they felt guilty, or isolated, or unsure of what to believe instead. But when asked, in effect, "Why not go back then?" they answered—almost without exception—that they simply could not make themselves believe what was unbelievable. They had concluded that what they had been taught all their lives was not true.

Where had this dedication to the truth come from? We concluded that, ironically, it had mainly resulted from the religious training itself. The family religion had been presented as the one, true religion. That made it wonderful: It was the Way, the Truth, and the Light. The children had also been taught to do the right thing, to have integrity. But when questions arose that could not be answered, the commitment to the home religion came in second to the commitment to truth. And they had trouble accepting things "on faith" because their well-developed personal integrity meant they had to believe what they professed. They were trapped, as some of them said, and had no other choice. So as a first cause, their upbringing was not repudiated by their apostasy but startlingly fulfilled by it.

Why, then, do so few persons who were emphatically told they belonged to the *true* religion abandon all faith? Their religion may not fail the test in most people's

Exhibit 3.1
The Religious Emphasis Scale

_____ 1. Emphasize attending religious services as acts of personal devotion?

_____ 2. Review the teachings of the religion at home?

_____ 3. Make religion the center, the most important part of your life?

_____ 4. Emphasize that you should read scriptures or other religious materials?

_____ 5. Discuss moral "dos" and "don'ts" in religious terms?

_____ 6. Make it clear that about the worst thing you could do in life would be to abandon your religion?

_____ 7. Stress being a good representative of your faith, who acted the way a devout member of your religion was expected to act?

_____ 8. Teach you that your religion's rules about morality were absolutely right, not to be questioned?

_____ 9. Tell you how wonderful it would be in heaven for all eternity?

_____ 10. Teach you that your religion was the truest religion, closest to God?

_____ 11. Stress that it was your responsibility to fight Satan all your life?

_____ 12. Impress upon you that unrepentant sinners would burn in hell for all eternity?

_____ 13. Make religion relevant to almost all aspects of your life?

_____ 14. Tell you how wrong it was to sin against a loving God?

_____ 15. Have you pray before bedtime?

_____ 16. Teach you to _strictly_ obey the commandments of almighty God?

_____ 17. Teach you that persons who tried to change the meaning of scripture and religious laws were evil and doing the devil's work?

_____ 18. Get you to do many "extra" religious acts so that the family religion "filled your life"?

_____ 19. Make a personal commitment to God as your only hope and savior?

_____ 20. Teach you to obey the persons who acted as God's representatives, such as priests, ministers, or rabbis?

Figure 3.1

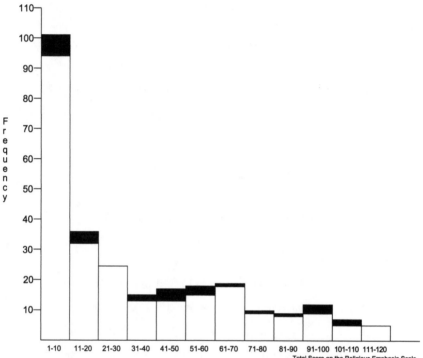

Distribution of Childhood Religious Emphasis Scores among San Francisco and Alabama/Idaho Atheists

Note: The frequency of the 28 Alabama/Idaho atheists is shown in the shaded portion at the top of each column. The rest of the column represents the 253 atheists from the San Francisco Area sample.

eyes. It may bring comfort, companionship, and other rewards that shush the doubts. The parental emphasis may carry a double message: (1) This is the truth, and (2) you better believe it! So they may have been too afraid to break away. But also, many people may not care as much about the issues. Our Amazing Apostates had usually been quite devout earlier in their lives, and still cared a great deal about religious issues. If they had cared less, if their home religion had not fostered a strong drive for the truth and integrity in them, and if they had not overcome their fear of going it alone, they probably would not have quit it.

A second cause also became evident during the interviews. The Amazing Apostates seemed quite bright. They had been good students in school; all but three said they had gotten above average marks. They had clearly been getting "the right answer" for years in their studies. They may thus have been more driven than most to finding the right answer to THE question. They may have been more capable of finding flaws in traditional teachings, and more likely to have the gumption (or in some eyes, hubris) to decide for themselves.[4]

Such people are rare. We asked the thousands of students in the total study if they had ever had doubts about their family religion. To our surprise, most said yes, including those from strong religious backgrounds. But in most of these latter cases they simply dropped the questions, or resolved them in their religion's favor. They tended to search for answers from sources (e.g., parents and ministers) likely to confirm the existing beliefs. Their search seemed as much for reassurance as anything else. In contrast, those with weak religious histories tended to search more widely, and to critically examine traditional beliefs; and their questions became active doubts. So also did our forty-six Amazing Apostates, who usually read up on other religions, the history of their own, and even studied atheism. This wider search, their dedication to discovering the truth, their commitment to integrity and being whatever it might be, and being smart enabled them to overcome all the social and family pressure to keep on believing—although some of them never revealed their apostasy to others.

"HOW I BECAME AN ATHEIST": FORTY CASES

But these were Canadian student apostates, not active American atheists with a median age of sixty. Do the findings apply to the cases at hand? We invited the American atheists to tell us their life stories, vis-à-vis religion, and have summarized forty of their histories below.[5] The first twenty come from that 50 percent of the sample whose Religious Emphasis scores equaled 20 or less. The last twenty come from the much more interesting 10 percent at other end of figure 3.1, from "Amazing Atheists" whose Emphasis scores exceeded 80. The cases in both sets are presented in the order in which the surveys came in. All are from the San Francisco sample unless otherwise noted. Take a look at them all. See what themes come up more often than others.

Twenty Active Atheists from Nonreligious Backgrounds

1. This fifty-one-year-old male grew up in a nominal Catholic family that made only token efforts to raise him in that faith. He nevertheless believed in God until age eight. "I thought of religion as a source of wisdom and morality. When I started catechism classes, preparing for confirmation, I found the priests and nuns less a model of virtue than my parents. I saw nuns criticize kids in class for not performing a religious requirement until they cried. I thought this was abuse. It made me angry. They also rejected findings of science, like evolution." By age ten the respondent had stopped believing in God. As you would suppose, this did not produce much tension in his family relations.

2. This contributor to our investigation, a sixty-nine-year-old male, had Protestant parents who had him pray to God before bedtime as he was growing up, but did little else religiously. He never felt religious, and doubts about God's existence developed during his midteens. No particular event or experience fueled his disbe-

lief. Instead the move to atheism "was easy and obvious, the only logical one for me." He worked the whole thing out by himself. His parents had a somewhat negative reaction when he announced he was dropping the family religion, but later "got over it." He resents people who consider him a "lost soul who would be a better person if I had some faith in the divine."

3. A sixty-two-year-old female who was raised a Lutheran, but whose major religious instruction merely involved occasional reminders of how wonderful heaven would be, this atheist began seriously to doubt God's existence at the age of thirteen. "It didn't make sense any more, especially the notion that only God can make sense out of contradictions." She did not discuss the issue with anyone, and even "decided to join my friends in the instruction before you are confirmed, giving religion one last chance." But the logical difficulties remained, and while still thirteen she concluded there is no God. Being an atheist has not caused her any problems in her family relations or elsewhere in life.

4. This respondent, a sixty-year-old woman who grew up in Europe in a family that never mentioned religion, only heard about God in school during instruction in the state religion. She said that her father told her, "Religion is a bunch of baloney," and that was about the extent of her religious instruction. "I never took it seriously— just another subject at school, more boring than most." She never had a religious impulse in her life, nor any doubts about her doubts "because I thought it was all stupid and ridiculous." Always an agnostic, she became an atheist at age twenty. It has cost her nothing, and she is quite proud of being so.

5. A fifty-five-year-old male, this nonbeliever grew up in a Methodist home where moderate emphasis was placed on going to church and aspects of religious morality, but little else. He believed in God, off and on, from his early teens to his midthirties, but the belief eventually vanished. Reading Bertrand Russell particularly influenced him. What finally made him an atheist? Getting to know a *theist* well. "After years of being mostly 'faithless,' I got to know a devout Christian. We became friends and spent many hours discussing religion. I saw clearly how his belief was grounded in fear of death. I knew I could not make decisions based on fear. I started calling myself an agnostic about age thirty, and an atheist last year." His changing beliefs may have affected his marriage: "I think one of the reasons my wife left me was because I did *not* become suddenly religious when my mother died."

6. This sixty-five-year-old man was raised a Methodist but answered the Religious Emphasis scale with a series of 0s and 1s. Nevertheless he considered himself religious until the age of thirteen, when (unspecified) doubts began to arise in his mind. He did not discuss these with anyone, but instead "I read and *thought*." In college he read *Man and His God* by Homer W. Smith, "and that finally did it." He became an atheist at twenty-one. He has not paid a price for this decision. "My parents were, and my friends are, highly intelligent, and therefore they understood."

7. Like many other respondents, this sixty-four-year-old male received no religious instruction in youth. "Religion was never discussed." "I never had any belief," he wrote, "and around 9 or 10 formalized atheist ideas." No particular event caused

this, "there was nothing to decide; it was obvious," and his lack of religious faith has cost him no problems with family, friends, or associates.

8. This participant, a sixty-four-year-old female, was nominally raised a Catholic but answered all the Emphasis items with a 0. She wrote, "I didn't realize my family was so unreligiously oriented." She considered herself religious until she was fifteen, when she became friends with a Christian Scientist and discovered another viewpoint. Keeping her questions to herself, she did "a great deal of reading over a lot of years" before deciding at about forty that she was an atheist. She did not care what friends or relatives thought about it, but does note that "anything I wanted to accomplish I would myself have to accomplish with no help from anyone or thing. If plans don't go my way I have no one to blame but myself."

9. A forty-eight-year-old male who also received absolutely no religious instruction in youth, this atheist was nonetheless religious as a child. "I off and on went to friends' churches, and assumed all this stuff must be true. On the other hand, I found out at age five that Santa Claus didn't exist, and I noticed the similarity of God to Santa Claus. Then my parents invited Fundamentalists to our house when I was twelve, and my Unitarian grandpa gave me a book about the Scopes 'Monkey Trial,' which led to a mini-Scopes trial at our house and the vanquishing of the evangelists. Plus I had Jewish friends whose parents were in Nazi camps. I decided, 'If God could allow this to happen, I wanted nothing to do with him.'" The respondent read extensively about evolution and science, enjoyed skeptic magazines, and decided at age forty he was an atheist. "But I keep quiet about it. People assume you're heartless, shallow, amoral, and it calls their own beliefs into question. Atheism *greatly* disturbs people."

10. This forty-three-year-old male respondent had an agnostic father and received absolutely no religious instruction as a child. "I was left to decide for myself." Nevertheless when he was very young he decided there was a God. He went to church with some friends, but as early as age eight began to raise questions and not get answers. "I tried praying as well—but it was pretty pointless." As an adolescent he "became curious and started reading religious texts and attending services. But questions again arose and [he] found all the answers unsatisfactory." At nineteen, he decided on atheism. His beliefs have produced strain with some relatives and friends, and have seriously affected his personal love life. "I think society as a whole views atheists as 'wrong people.' We are a minority that it is still all right to treat as second-class citizens and bash verbally."

11. An eighty-year-old male, this eventual atheist was raised in the Church of Christ in a very minimal way. "My parents attended church and I was expected to attend while I was young. But religion was seldom if ever discussed at home. Belief in God disappeared when the Santa Claus myth was revealed. I heard tales of angels flitting around in the sky, somebody sitting on a throne in the sky, somebody watching all the time, pearly gates and heaven for all the good people, and I thought, 'Here we go again.'" But the respondent kept his conclusions to himself. "I followed the paths of my peers—baptized at about eleven, attended Sunday school, memo-

rized passages from the Bible. But I stopped going at about fourteen. I read about science and the history of religions. But I seldom if ever discuss my religion with relatives or friends, who probably do not know my beliefs."

12. This thirty-eight-year-old male was raised a Catholic but answered 0 to all the Emphasis items but one. One parent was an agnostic. Serious doubts about religion arose early, "at age 8 when I was about to make my first communion. I had to go to confession. I couldn't understand why I had to talk to a priest in order to talk to God." He asked his parents, who told him to do what the other children were doing. Thereafter he kept his doubts to himself. He did not mention doing any reading on the subject. "In high school I just decided I didn't believe in God. I was at a Catholic high school too!" He did not tell anyone about this until after 9/11, however. "Some friends were shocked, especially those who have known me a long time. I never realized how negative being an atheist is until recently. I don't talk about my beliefs."

13. Raised an Episcopalian in name only, this fifty-six-year-old woman came to believe in God when she was in her twenties. Then her sister died. "I could not reconcile myself to the fact that an 'all-loving God' would make her suffer like she did. I read a small book in the library on atheism and it made complete sense to me." Being an atheist has not cost her anything. "Once I explain that I am happy and content with my beliefs, people generally leave me alone."

14. A fifty-six-year-old male, this nonbeliever was raised a Seventh-day Adventist but his Religious Emphasis score equaled zero. Nevertheless he immersed himself in the Bible and Adventist literature as a child, and considers himself to have been quite religious until age twelve. Doubts had arisen a few years earlier due to nature classes at a local museum, and he then immersed himself in "the 590 Dewey Decimal System books at the public library." He became an atheist at twelve, he wrote, "when it came to me that Christians don't literally believe, but conform and act as on a stage. Most never think of the issues unless in dire straits when it becomes a 'Get out of jail FREE' card. The disillusionment—like losing belief in Santa Claus—was intense. But in the United States the default state is 'believer.' I learned to never assert atheism. It's sort of like burning the flag."

15. This forty-eight-year-old male received only a token education in Judaism as both parents were nonbelievers. He never considered himself religious, saw many contradictions in religious teachings, and "after going through Jewish confirmation, I told my parents that religion was a bunch of bunk and hypocritical." The parents agreed, and explained they had sent him to religious school so he could make a choice. He has not paid a price for his atheism, except "perhaps no inclusion in religious social events."

16. A sixty-nine-year-old female, this respondent received a very minimal introduction to the Lutheran faith because both of her parents were agnostics. Still, she believed in God as a child. Then, "when I was 13 and in confirmation class, I started to think it was ridiculous that a god impregnated a human. I told the minister I wouldn't be confirmed unless he could prove to me Christ was divine. I got the usual

lecture on faith and created a scandal when I stood my ground. But my dad said, 'OK.' I stopped going to church and never worried about it." She became an atheist in her thirties and has not paid any price personally or socially for her beliefs. "But we chose to live in the San Francisco Bay area where all sorts of odd or un-American notions are both tolerated and encouraged."

17. A fifty-five-year-old woman of Jewish background, this respondent received minimal instruction in Judaism as she was growing up. Yet for a while, around nine or ten, she felt devout and would say a bedtime prayer. Then she read *The Diary of Anne Frank*, which, with personal experiences, led her to conclude life was unfair and arbitrary. She thought her parents were hypocritical for making her go to Saturday school and making her observe major holiday services, when they were not religious at all. At age twenty-three she realized she was not an agnostic but an atheist. Since then she has felt tension with some friends, and misses being able to take comfort in a "greater meaning" when things go wrong or seem unfair.

18. This respondent, a thirty-seven-year-old man in the Alabama/Idaho study, had a minimal introduction to the Presbyterian faith. But he says he was never religious. "It seemed so 'hocus-pocus' and was full of contradictions and inconsistencies. As a child I read the Bible, Qu'ran, Torah, and other books and was able to identify the nonsense contained therein. It made me wonder what was wrong with adults if a child could figure it out." Studying the Bible at age thirteen made him decide on atheism. He went on to say, "To this day my in-laws consider me the 'anti-Christ' and refuse to talk to me. Other relatives took a long time to accept my atheism and some are still weary of having me around, especially around their children. I have had crosses planted in my yard, my kids have been harassed at school, I've been a victim of religious discrimination at work, my car has been vandalized, I've received death threats via email, mail and under my windshield wipers. The neighborhood adults think it necessary to teach my children about God and Jesus when my kids are at their house, yet they would have a heart attack if I talked religion to their kids (I don't). I've lost over $200 in bumper stickers and decals that have been ripped off my car. I've spent over $500 repairing damage to my vehicle because of vandalism."

19. This forty-seven-year-old female from the Alabama/Idaho sample was raised an atheist by atheist parents and was one of the very few respondents who said she was taught as a child that religion was wrong and should be rejected. She decided on atheism at age eight. This has cost her some friends and some jobs, and she has learned to be discreet about her religious views.

20. This seventy-five-year-old man from the Alabama/Idaho sample was not raised in any religion, but felt a religious impulse at age eleven that led him to study Christianity. But as he studied and recited the catechism, serious doubts arose "in my head from reasoning." When he was fourteen he decided he was an atheist. He became a doctor, but his beliefs cost him a lot of patients. He was "vilified and essentially asked to get off the board of a humane society peopled mostly by fundamentalists."

Twenty Active Atheists from Very Religious Backgrounds

21. A sixty-four-year-old male, this future atheist recounted that he was raised a strict Catholic, answering 6 to every item on the Religious Emphasis scale. At his father's behest he became a priest, but during his thirties found it intellectually difficult to maintain his beliefs. He joined the Jesus Seminar in an attempt to find the historical Jesus, but remained a priest until his father died. He left the order and the church at his father's funeral. He has paid a heavy price for this break. "I have no family now."

22. A seventy-two-year-old female, this ex-Catholic said she was "very religious through my childhood, but began to question in my twenties, had doubts in my thirties, was an apostate at 40 and an atheist at 60. The first thing I noticed was that the most devout were so hypocritical. The men were having extra-marital affairs, and women were so critical of others. I did a lot of reading about religion, history and philosophy." But taking physics and astronomy classes decided the matter for her. She has not paid much of a price "because I don't make a big issue of it. But my family is aware that I don't go to church anymore."

23. A seventy-year-old ex-Baptist, this respondent said he never believed what he was taught about God. "I was to believe God is omnipotent, omnipresent and *good*, yet he did nothing to alleviate or stop suffering." He asked his grandparents and Sunday school teacher for answers, but found them "nonsensical, such as it is sometimes hard to understand the Lord." He quit the church when he was thirteen. This put quite a strain on his relationships with various members of his family, and he has lost romantic attachments "because I didn't believe in the god of the ladies I was dating."

24. This forty-seven-year-old female firmly believed her Baptist faith until the time she graduated from high school. She had sex with her boyfriend then, and felt very guilty about it, but then wondered why she should feel that way. She did a lot of soul-searching, and took classes in the humanities in college "and [her] practical nature" led her to become an atheist by twenty-eight. But she kept this from her parents for a very long time.

25. A former fundamentalist who also maxed out on the Religious Emphasis scale, this forty-two-year-old female believed her home religion until her early twenties. Then it seemed to her that the church's treatment of women and gays was wrong, and the Bible was full of contradictory stories that seemed absurd. She spent several years pondering these matters, eventually deciding she was an atheist around the age of twenty-five. This decision ended many relationships with family members and friends.

26. This sixty-seven-year-old male was raised a Baptist and believed the teachings of his home religion until age twenty. However, as he proselytized his faith, people asked him questions that he had a hard time answering. He asked other religious people for their answers, and their common response was to not question the faith, but instead to pray. He then looked for answers in the Bible "but only found

more things that were impossible to believe." Praying for guidance seemed "like talking into a telephone with a dead line." Around the age of twenty-two he ceased to believe in God. This has cost him a lot. He nearly committed suicide, lost his Christian friends, and hurt his relatives. He also has lost "having all the answers and looking forward to an everlasting life in heaven."

27. A forty-year-old male who was raised a Seventh-day Adventist, this contributor began to have serious doubts about his religion at age eighteen. He spoke to no one about these, but instead read books. William James and Bertrand Russell particularly influenced him. Then a pastor of the Worldwide Church of God allowed his five-year-old son to die without medical help, and this convinced him that religious beliefs were preposterous. He has never told his family, and misses old friends who know and now shun him.

28. This sixty-three-year-old respondent began to have doubts about his strong Baptist upbringing at age ten. He revealed this to a peer who was so horrified that he recanted and kept his doubts to himself for many years. In the early 1960s a *Time* magazine story titled "God Is Dead" shocked him and he sought guidance from his minister. The latter told him the story was referring to the fact that God was dead in most of society's actions. But he began reading and attending lectures on religion. "By then I had given myself permission to hold my own opinions." He was an atheist by thirty. The change has produced "no real stress, but not much conversation either."

29. This thirty-seven-year-old female was raised a strong Baptist, and her faith held firm ("with the occasional re-interpretation of scripture") until her twenties. Then, during a casual debate with a friend, she relates, "At one point I had no idea whether the next thing to leave my mouth was true or not! The shock of that realization was the beginning of the end." It took a year or so to get over that shock and to realize that "I didn't believe any of it anymore. Life just made a lot more sense. Telling my folks was scary, but I'm glad I did. It's given me much more than it's cost me."

30. Raised a Catholic, this forty-one-year-old male accepted his thoroughly taught religious beliefs until he was twenty. Then he began to wonder why Jesus' crucifixion would/could have been a "necessary human atonement." He also came to accept his homosexuality, which put him at odds with his church. Reflection on the "first cause" proof of God's existence led to its rejection. He read books on atheism, and eventually found the traditional arguments for God's existence unconvincing. By thirty-six he decided he was an atheist. This has not cost him much because most of his family does not know.

31. This seventy-one-year-old man grew up in "a 100% Catholic region in Europe where everything was under the strict control of the church." At age ten he asked a teacher about a contradiction in their faith and was given an angry rebuke and punishment. He kept his doubts to himself after that, but over time believed less and less. When he came to the United States at thirty, he embraced the freedom to believe what he wanted, and was an atheist by thirty-two. This has caused little difficulty with his family, who also has lost their religiousness as the Catholic Church's influence has dissipated in their region. But being outspoken about his beliefs has

caused problems. "When I wear a t-shirt with an atheist slogan, I get a verbal attack. I've had to remove an atheist sticker from the rear of my scooter because car drivers would try to run me off the road, screaming 'Jesus is the Lord.' And police would pull me over and check my papers for no reason."

32. This forty-six-year-old female accepted her strong Baptist training until her early twenties. Then, she says, she began to recognize "my family's disrespect for women, based on religion, and all other religions' misogyny. My family's religion allowed them to treat me as less of a person than my non-religious friends did." She had many discussions about this with her friends, and about the age of thirty openly became an atheist. This caused big problems with her parents. "My non-religious 'coming-out' was far worse than a gay friend's coming out to his parents. It took 8 years to get a better relationship with my parents. I have to be very careful with my co-workers and a couple of my friends."

33. This fifty-eight-year-old nonbeliever wrote that he believed his Church of Christ upbringing "from earliest memory until completion of college." But he majored in Religious Studies, and was impressed by the theology of Paul Tillich. He discussed the impact this was having on his own beliefs with no one, relying instead on "rational thought." At twenty-two he became an atheist. This has produced "some strain" with his family.

34. This fifty-five-year-old female was given strong training in the Catholic Church, which she accepted for thirty years. At age thirty-two, however, she began to have doubts (but she did not say what triggered them). She read widely and concluded that discoveries in evolution and biochemistry undermined much of her faith. Also, "a personal depression" occurred "wherein I realized that religion relies on and fosters pain." She then became an atheist. Her mother was upset, and as a result the respondent lost her inheritance.

35. A sixty-four-year-old male from the Alabama/Idaho sample of our study, this respondent was given such a strong upbringing in the Church of Christ that, despite doubts that began when he was nineteen, his faith endured almost all his life. The questions began when his study of the synoptic Gospels (Mark, Matthew, and Luke) revealed "the irresolvable contradictions therein." He asked his ministers and Bible teachers for guidance, and was told, "You need more faith." However, further reading revealed "even more contradictions in scripture. The rigidity of preachers and their emphasis on building their own reputation" led him eventually (very eventually) to become an atheist at sixty-two. "Being an atheist activist has made some believers afraid of me. They know they cannot answer hard questions well."

36. Raised a Baptist, this sixty-three-year-old male from the Alabama/Idaho sample accepted his home religion until he was fifteen. However, at about age thirteen serious doubts arose when he was told, "The unforgivable sin was to doubt or question." Rather than stifle his questions, this warning led him to read science books and articles, especially about dinosaurs and evolution. At sixteen he read the novel *Elmer Gantry*, and this influenced him further. At that age he ceased to believe in God. His atheism has put a strain between himself and his relatives and friends,

and he had to turn down "a rather handsome job offer because I would have been expected to participate in community clubs and attend church."

37. This eighty-two-year-old male from the Alabama/Idaho sample was given a strong upbringing in the Baptist faith, which he believed until age twenty-nine. However, doubts began to arise when he was twenty-seven, caused by "World War II, and the discovery that Paul's Christianity was a myth." This led to extensive reading of the Bible and the writings of scholars. Eventually the inconsistency within scripture and the "obvious anthropomorphic nature of biblical claims" resulted in his atheism at twenty-nine. This caused great tension with relatives, but not with certain friends.

38. A seventy-one-year-old female from the Alabama/Idaho sample, this respondent grew up in the Church of Christ and maintained her faith until she was twenty-five. However, doubts began to arise when she realized that "at age 18 girls could write a program for 'Young People's Meeting,' but only boys could orally present it. Women were to be silent in the church." She began to read more widely, and was particularly influenced by Crane Brinton's *The Shaping of the Modern Mind*. Biblical contradictions and discoveries about the origins of scripture led her to decide on atheism at age twenty-seven. Her parents disassociated themselves from her for years, believing it was their duty to do so. They later came together, but religion was not discussed. When her husband divorced her, he pled that "my religious direction warranted a label of being considered 'mentally unbalanced.'"

39. This thirty-four-year-old male from the Alabama/Idaho sample was given a solid Catholic upbringing that hit a bump at age ten when he asked his parents, "Why, if we are to love all, are we not to love those outside our religion?" The parents' response was unsatisfying, which led the boy to study other religions and read many books. He decided "no one is right, but maybe no one is wrong." He became an atheist at age twenty-four, but has kept his views to himself for nearly a decade.

40. The youngest person in the study, this eighteen-year-old male from the Alabama/Idaho sample was given a strong Christian education, but he says it never "took." "I tried and tried to find absolute faith, to be caught up in the religious 'rapture' of those I knew, but I just never felt anything. I can remember being 7 years old and questioning parts of the Baptist services I went to." He decided he could not believe in God at age fourteen. "It seriously strains some of my relationships, especially with my very conservative Christian family. Total strangers sometimes insult me for my pentacle."

ANALYSIS OF THE ORIGINS OF THE SAMPLES' ATHEISM

So, what did you notice from these various accounts? First of all, were you as surprised as we were at how often these confirmed atheists had once gone through a "religious period" in their lives—even the ones who received minimal religious socialization? Looking at all the cases, 76 percent of the San Francisco sample and

71 percent of those from Alabama/Idaho stated they once believed in God. Would you have guessed that from figure 3.1? But in retrospect, does not nearly everyone wonder, at some point, "Where did the world come from?" and "What happens to us when we die?" In America, where strong majorities believe in God and an afterlife, the cultural answers surround a youth growing up in a nonreligious home. Sometimes friends, grandparents, or neighbors will take the child to church; sometimes the child just picks up religious beliefs on her own from the social milieu. Typically this religiousness begins in middle childhood (median age of eight in the Bay Area sample, seven among the Alabama/Idaho participants) and lasts some time. Typically, the nonreligious parents do not mind, just as we found that very few nonreligious parents ever preached against religion.[6]

Then, in the San Francisco sample, serious doubts erupted during adolescence (median age of fifteen, but with an incredible range of five to fifty). In Alabama and Idaho, the doubts appeared later, with a median of eighteen, and a range of ten to forty-two. A few times the questions arose because of some personal tragedy or disappointment. But mostly, in both samples, as in our study of Canadian student apostates, the questions arose over ideas, which confirms what we saw in the Doubts Scale data in chapter 2. More than anything else, future atheists said reading the Bible started them wondering. Learning about evolution or astronomy was also mentioned with some frequency. Now and then someone said the writings of Bertrand Russell or some other atheist had started them questioning. The problem of evil troubled some. Observation of hypocrisy in churchgoers bothered others. Teachings on sex and gender roles started a few on the road to atheism. A few began to wonder about Satan and exorcisms. Several stated, as you probably noticed, that their doubts about God had begun when they learned there was no Santa Claus. Others doubted medical "miracles," or "bleeding statues," or TV evangelists. Still others wondered why tornados sometimes flattened churches but missed "houses of sin." Some realized all religions could not be right, so maybe none of them was. Some mentioned religious intolerance or teachings about homosexuality. A few said their questions had grown from learning about the history of Christianity, the Crusades, pogroms, and so on. Still others said they simply realized there was no proof of their religious beliefs, so why believe? Belief, in short, bled through multiple wounds but the letting typically flowed for intellectual, not emotional or personal reasons.

How Did the American Atheists Drop Their Religious Beliefs?

As mentioned earlier in this chapter, Canadian students at least commonly go through a period of religious questioning and doubt during adolescence, but only those who make a determined search of both sides of the issue tend to lose their faith. The active American atheists appear to have searched for answers about God's existence and been underwhelmed by the case for theism. Where did they search? How long did it take?

The road to disbelief for these atheists did not run through a Young Disbelievers

Club or a Campus Crusade Against Christ. Most (77 percent in the Bay Area sample, 72 percent in the Alabama/Idaho group) said they did not ask anyone for help or advice about their doubts but instead thought things out on their own, turning to books rather than peers. (Those who *did* ask parents, priests, and so on for help obviously found no satisfying answers.) The process was not decided overnight for those who had been taught or who had picked up religious beliefs. On the average, San Francisco atheists chose atheism at age twenty-one—six years after serious doubts had arisen. The median age in Alabama and Idaho, where the consequences of atheism loomed large, equaled thirty-two, a solid fourteen years of considering doubts that had begun at eighteen. Again the ranges proved huge: one person from the San Francisco sample said he had been an atheist from the age of seven; another had his first doubts at thirty-six but only became an atheist at sixty-five. The "study period" was even longer for some Alabama/Idaho respondents, three of whom had their first serious doubts during their teen years, but only became atheists in their fifties. For persons from very religious families, or those living in staunchly religious parts of the country, becoming an atheist could mean permanent separation and ostracism.[7] It would be a path taken most thoughtfully.

Were you as astonished as we were by the number of atheists who reported they had paid a significant price for their (non) beliefs? Even in the San Francisco area—arguably the most tolerant part of the United States—most of that sample (53 percent) reported that being a nonbeliever had produced difficulty with relatives and friends. The figure was predictably higher (67 percent) and the price often far greater in Alabama and Idaho.

Then why did these atheists *choose* to become members of a vilified minority? We tried to ask this question most directly on the survey as follows:

> Many people find great comfort in religion. It tells them the purpose of their lives. It helps them deal with pain and suffering. It lessens their fear of death, and indeed promises them life eternal. It tells them what is right and wrong. It provides an anchor, explains mysteries, and makes them feel safe. And it seems to pay off in various ways. For example, several well-controlled studies have found that, on the average, persons who attend church frequently live longer than those who do not.
>
> If you are an atheist or an agnostic, you probably realized all or most of this long ago. And yet you turn your back on all these benefits. Why? What makes your position so worthwhile that you give up all this? Why can't you believe what most people find it very natural and easy to believe?

The answers we got to this "hard question" took many forms, and a few of our respondents wrote that we must be trying to convert them to theism. But most of the active atheists essentially replied, "Because it is all so unbelievable!" Like our Canadian Amazing Apostates, these confirmed atheists simply could not make themselves believe what most people believe. It was all too flawed, too self-contradictory, too unsupported, too illogical they said. They wanted the Truth. As one of them wrote, "My mother believes with all her heart that Satan turned me away, but it was the

Bible. Nobody brainwashed me or led me into a cult. I studied my church's teachings and that's what made me stop believing."

Such are not, by the way, the usual reasons people give for dropping the family religion. As we saw in the introduction, a survey of over four hundred parents of students at the University of Manitoba who said they had not passed on the family religion to their children found that hypocrisy, boring services, a constant request for money, and changing social norms all deadened fervor more than "I could not agree with certain important teachings of my religion" or "The religious teachings I was taught seem contradictory and don't make much sense. I didn't want to pass them on."[8]

So what made getting the truth so important to these American atheists? They would probably say, "You're asking the wrong question of the wrong people. Why do believers believe what can't be proven?" But still, we want to know what made these atheists so different from the mainstream.

The primary explanation must lay in figure 3.1, in the general lack of religious instruction in their youths. True, we did not anticipate how often "un-indoctrinated" children still went through a religious period. But their faith likely had shallow roots, and as we saw in the first twenty case descriptions, there was seldom anyone in their families to pressure them, explicitly or implicitly, to believe in God when doubts arose.

But what about the "amazing atheists" from the second batch of case descriptions, the ones who came from very religious backgrounds? Their answers sounded to us a lot like those of the Amazing Apostates from our 1994–1995 study. They usually believed ardently for some time, but then an issue arose or some doubt flared up that they could not answer satisfactorily. And it was necessary *to them* that an adequate answer be found, that integrity be maintained, that their religion live up to the high standards *it* had taught them as they were growing up. When an appreciable period of thinking, reading, and searching showed it could not, the once true believer stopped believing. As with the earlier Amazing Apostates, the devil did not make them do it—their religious upbringing did, we think.

Beyond this, it takes some brainpower and critical reasoning skills to tear Aquinas asunder, to notice that Cain feared "anyone" would kill him as he wandered the supposedly unpopulated earth, to understand science, to comprehend Bertrand Russell while a teenager, and so on. These atheists appear quite intelligent. They went to school a lot, with the Bay Area participants averaging seventeen years of formal education and the Alabama/Idaho respondents sixteen. Most of them had graduated from college—not all that common a triumph for persons (mostly) born in the 1940s—and many had gone on to graduate school. Highly intelligent children, the sort likely to attend university later, are rewarded over and over again for getting "the right answer" as they grow up. And they may come to value getting the right answer so much that they will pay a significant price rather than settle for something that does not make sense to them.[9]

The question might then arise, are there collateral costs, shared with firmly convinced theists, for being that sure you are right? Are active atheists dogmatic, zealous, and prejudiced?

NOTES

1. B. Spilka, R. W. Hood, B. Hunsberger, and R. Gorsuch, *The Psychology of Religion: An Empirical Approach*, 3rd ed. (New York: Guilford Press, 2003), chap. 5.

2. The San Francisco mean equaled 31.8 with a standard deviation of 32.6. The Alabama/Idaho mean of 43.8 (36.9) was significantly higher: $t = 2.16$, $p < 0.05$. The mean inter-item correlation of the Religious Emphasis items equaled 0.69 in the San Francisco sample and 0.70 among the Alabama/Idaho atheists, producing alphas of 0.98 in both cases. The Manitoba parents did not answer the Religious Emphasis items shown in table 4.1, but instead (for space reasons) answered only ten items, and on a 0 through 5 basis. Of course, the atheist parents came from significantly less religious backgrounds than the fundamentalist parents did (means of 9.7 vs. 31.2 respectively). But comparisons with the American data would be problematic.

3. Bob Altemeyer and Bruce Hunsberger, *Amazing Conversions: Why Some Turn to Faith and Others Abandon Religion* (Amherst, NY: Prometheus Books, 1997).

4. We also studied Canadian students who came from very nonreligious backgrounds but who had become very religious. In most cases this seemed to be a way of solving personal problems (e.g., the students had been lonely, or fighting addictions, or become afraid of death). They had not converted for theological reasons, but for emotional ones. Some of them were still finding out what their adopted religion taught. And in most cases they were led to their new faith by others, especially by peers through such things as youth groups run by the denomination.

5. A careful reader, the kind who reads the notes in a chapter, would be wondering now, Why *these* forty stories—especially in the case of the low Religious Emphasis scores when there are over one hundred individuals to chose from? In general, we picked cases that would show the range of circumstances and paths that led to atheism, leaving it to later summary statistics to indicate the most common factors in the sample as a whole. People are individuals, and it's nice to be able to tell different, individual stories as well as provide the necessary averages. As we did in our study of Amazing Conversions, we have sometimes changed facts about respondents' background, such as their gender or age to disguise their identity and preserve their anonymity. In no case do these changes materially affect the gist of the story being told. We have also omitted some parts of some responses that are off the topic of how the person became an atheist, and done light editorial work on spelling, expanding abbreviations, combining answers from different parts of the survey, and so on.

6. After seeing the Bay Area responses, we asked different sets of questions of those Alabama/Idaho atheists who said they had never been religious, as well as those who said they had. The former group of lifelong nonbelievers numbered only *eight*. For what it was worth, seven reported they were *not* taught as children to be nonreligious; most of them simply were not taught to *be* religious.

7. Especially in some parts of the country. The San Francisco Atheists Club has over one thousand names on its mailing list. The Alabama Atheists Club has ten.

8. See B. Altemeyer, "The Decline of Organized Religion in Western Civilization," *International Journal for the Psychology of Religion* 14 (2004): 77–89.

9. We are not saying, of course, that theists are stupid. Also, it is possible that a college education promotes atheism. But a longitudinal study at a large public Canadian university during the era when most of our active atheists would have been attending college found no net effect of higher education on religiousness. Some students became less religious over

time, but others became more so. Most of the students at the University of Manitoba who are nonbelievers when they graduate were nonbelievers when they entered. See B. Hunsberger, "The Religiosity of College Students: Stability and Change over Years at University," *Journal for the Scientific Study of Religion* 17 (1978): 159–64. (Mid)adolescence, more than any other age in life, appears to be the crucible for future religious belief, although final decisions are often not made for years.

CHAPTER 4

DOGMATISM

B y "dogmatism" we mean relatively unchangeable, unjustified certainty. And we are absolutely certain that this is the best-est definition there could possibly be. Nothing could convince us otherwise.

Well OK, the definition has some problems, particularly with the word *unjustified*. We often do not know the truth, and occasionally silly ideas, such as we go around the sun and not vice versa (all visual evidence to the contrary), turn out to be right. Also we tend to think that people who won't change their minds and agree with us are dogmatic, while those we are arguing with may well think the same about us—especially if it's one of those arguments in which people will make up any "fact" they need to win the fight. Each side may perceive the other's position as unjustified; very few people think that *they* are dogmatic, for heaven's sake.

Consequently, we often cannot say, in all fairness, whether someone's certainty is unjustified. But we can measure how open a person is to the possibility that she might be wrong and open to open-mindedness in general. Is it axiomatic that all rational, clear-headed people would agree with you, or is it possible that someone who disagrees could still be rational and clear-headed? Is doubt destructive? Do you see everything with perfect clarity, with everything fitting perfectly into place? Could your beliefs possibly change in the future? Could anything change your mind?

To measure these various aspects of dogmatism we developed a paper-and-pencil measure called the DOG scale, which we administered to all the participants in this study. You can see its twenty items in exhibit 4.1, and again feel free to answer it yourself now. Only note that: (a) the response scale runs from -4 to +4 rather than the 0 to 6 you used in the last two chapters; (b) half of the items are worded such that the dogmatic response is to agree, and half are worded such that a dogmatic person would disagree; and (c) you should not trust your answers, since you know the test is intended to measure dogmatism and nobody wants to appear dogmatic.

Exhibit 4.1
The DOG Scale

I. Please give your reactions to each of the statements below, according to the following scale:

–4 = Very strong disagreement	0 = Neutral or no opinion
–3 = Strong disagreement	+1 = Slight agreement
–2 = Moderate disagreement	+2 = Moderate agreement
–1 = Slight disagreement	+3 = Strong agreement
	+4 = Very strong agreement

_____ 1. Anyone who is honestly and truly seeking the truth will end up believing what I believe.

_____ 2. There are so many things we have not discovered yet, nobody should be absolutely certain his beliefs are right.

_____ 3. The things I believe in are so completely true, I could never doubt them.

_____ 4. I have never discovered a system of beliefs that explains everything to my satisfaction.

_____ 5. It is best to be open to all possibilities, and ready to reevaluate all your beliefs.

_____ 6. My opinions are right, and will stand the test of time.

_____ 7. Flexibility is a real virtue in thinking, since you may well be wrong.

_____ 8. My opinions and beliefs fit together perfectly to make a crystal-clear "picture" of things.

_____ 9. There are no discoveries or facts that could possibly make me change my mind about the things that matter most in life.

_____ 10. I am a long way from reaching final conclusions about the central issues in life.

_____ 11. The person who is absolutely certain she has the truth will probably never find it.

_____ 12. I am absolutely certain that my ideas about the fundamental issues in life are correct.

_____ 13. The people who disagree with me may well turn out to be right.

_____ 14. I am so sure I am right about the important things in life, there is no evidence that could convince me otherwise.

_____ 15. If you are "open-minded" about the most important things in life, you will probably reach the wrong conclusions.

_____ 16. Twenty years from now, some of my opinions about the important things in life will probably have changed.

_____ 17. "Flexibility in thinking" is another name for being "wishy-washy."

_____ 18. No one knows all the essential truths about the central issues in life.

_____ 19. Someday I will probably realize my present ideas about the BIG issues are wrong.

_____ 20. People who disagree with me are just plain wrong, and often evil as well.

Note: Responses are scored as follows. For Items 1, 3, 6, 8, 9, 12, 14, 15, 17, and 20, a -4 is coded as 1, a -3 is coded as 2, a -2 is coded as 3, a -1 is coded as 4, a 0 is coded as 5, a +1 is coded as 6, a +2 is coded as 7, a +3 is coded as 8, and a +4 is coded as 9. For the other items, the scoring key is reversed. That is, -4 is coded as 9, -3 is coded as 8, and so on up to +4 being coded as 1.

EVIDENCE FOR VALIDITY

Did you notice that the DOG scale makes no mention of religion? It was composed to capture dogmatism of any sort: scientific, religious, socialist, feminist, environmental, astrological, New Age, old age. Does it? In one study, university students indicated, in twelve different ways, how zealous they were about their "most important outlook in life"—whatever it was. For example, did they try to explain this outlook to others at every opportunity? Was nothing else as important in their life? Were they committed to making this outlook the strongest influence in the world? If we assume that, as a generalization, zealous people tend to be dogmatic, then the DOG scale does its job well because the more zealous people were about their most important outlook (whatever it was), the higher they also tended to score on the DOG scale. The study was then repeated with parents of university students, with the same result.[1] Incidentally, while a few zealous capitalists, socialists, environmentalists, and feminists showed up in the samples, persons championing religious beliefs had the highest zealot and highest DOG scores in both samples.

In another study relatively homophobic students were presented with some of the mounting evidence that sexual orientation has, to some extent, biological and even prenatal roots. Those hostile students who *also* had high DOG scores were *un*affected by these studies and maintained their negative attitudes. They responded in a closed-minded way. But those initially hostile students with low DOG scores shifted their attitudes markedly toward greater tolerance of gays and lesbians.

In a third study, students reacted to a hypothetical discovery of scientifically validated ancient scrolls that showed the story of Jesus had been largely borrowed from earlier Greek myths. Those who strongly believed Jesus was the divine son of God and who *also* had scored high in dogmatism indicated this discovery would have no effect whatsoever on their belief. On the other hand, students who believed just as strongly in Jesus' divinity, but who had scored low on the DOG scale, indicated this discovery would cause a major shift in their belief. So, as with hostility toward homosexuals, the higher the DOG scores, the more people would ignore scientific evidence when it disconfirmed their beliefs.

Finally, in a fourth study students who held that the Bible is free of any errors, contradictions, or inconsistencies were shown, side-by-side, the four Gospel accounts of Easter morning. The accounts contain numerous contradictions and inconsistencies about who discovered Jesus, how it happened, who else was around, what supernatural phenomena occurred, who was told of Jesus' reappearance, and so on. These were pointed out to the true believers, who were then asked to explain them. Those who had racked up high scores on the DOG scale still tended to insist, despite all, that the Bible contains no contradictions or inconsistencies. (They most commonly explained that the writers of the Gospels were telling the same story from different points of view, like witnesses to an automobile accident. This rationale, perhaps given in Sunday school, therefore *admits* that contradictions exist and merely describes how they arose.) The true believers who scored lower on the DOG scale, on the other hand, usually changed their stand and admitted contradictions exist. (They typically explained them as translation errors or allowed that the evangelists got some details wrong.)[2]

These four studies do not establish the validity of the DOG scale, which has only been around for a few years and is still a pup. Tomorrow research might appear that fails to replicate these findings in other populations, or finds no connection with other kinds of dogmatic behavior. But for the moment at least, the test does appear to measure "relatively unchangeable, unjustified certainty." We know that highly religious persons tend to have high scores on the measure and to be dogmatic in a number of ways. So what are we going to find when atheists put down their answers to the items in exhibit 4.1?

Figure 4.1 shows the median DOG scores of the San Francisco Atheists, the Alabama/Idaho atheists, the atheist Manitoba parents, and the Manitoba parents who had very high scores in religious fundamentalism. The least dogmatic response possible to each statement on the DOG scale is coded as a 1, so the minimum possible score on the test would be (20 × 1 =) 20. The most dogmatic response possible is coded as a 9, making the maximum possible score (20 × 9 =) 180. A score of 100 would plop halfway between these extremes. The Canadian student and parent samples we gather for most of our studies usually have an overall mean of 70-something, indicating, in absolute terms, low levels of dogmatism. The American atheists in this study averaged 88, which startled us because nonbelievers in Manitoba samples have always ranked among the least dogmatic groups one could find. You can see in figure 4.1 that the parent atheists we tested for this study posted a median of 65. Still, all these atheists look pretty undogmatic compared with the fundamentalist Manitoba parents, who slam-dunked a 126.[3]

Why did the American atheists score as high as they did? We have to cut them some slack here because they have celebrated about a dozen more birthdays than the Manitoba parents. So items such as "Someday I will probably realize my present ideas about the BIG issues are wrong," "I am a long way from reaching final conclusions about the central issues in life," and "Twenty years from now, some of my opinions about the important things in life will probably have changed" probably mean something a little different to a person who is sixty than they do to one who is forty-eight.

Nevertheless the American atheists gave more dogmatic answers to *all* of the items on the DOG scale than did the Manitoba parent atheists—and the difference was statistically significant in nearly every case. Besides the age-related items mentioned above, the San Francisco and Alabama/Idaho atheists gave particularly dogmatic answers to "Anyone who is honestly and truly seeking the truth will end up believing what I believe," "The things I believe in are so completely true, I could never doubt them," and "My opinions and beliefs fit together perfectly to make a crystal-clear 'picture' of things." Even allowing that the American atheists' average fell on the *un*dogmatic side of 100, these sentiments still gave us pause. Perhaps we should have realized that persons able to conclude that the vast majority of human

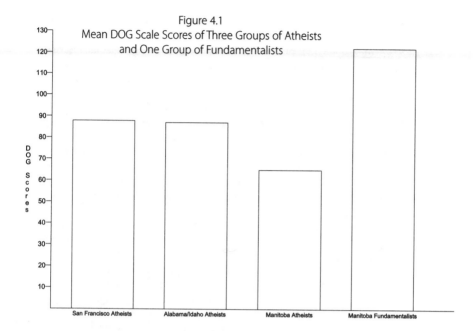

Figure 4.1
Mean DOG Scale Scores of Three Groups of Atheists
and One Group of Fundamentalists

kind and human history has been wrong about God would be relatively certain of their beliefs in general.

THE "ANCIENT SCROLLS" EXPERIMENT

Answers to the DOG scale may reveal dogmatic attitudes but they do not constitute dogmatic *behavior*. To assess behavior we presented two other situations in the booklet. First, remember the ancient-scrolls narrative we used to measure closed-mindedness among Christians who were asked how their beliefs would be affected if sound, scientific evidence showed Jesus had never existed? We had also developed a parallel scenario that asked nonbelievers how they would react to ancient scrolls that supported the existence and divinity of Jesus. We found most Manitoba student nonbelievers said such a discovery *would* shift their belief, indicating an open-mindedness on the matter.[4] We accordingly put this "Ancient Scroll" proposition in the booklets filled out by two of our atheist samples (dropping it from the Alabama/Idaho booklet to save space).

The procedure began with a request that the person react to the following statement on a -4 to +4 basis: "Jesus of Nazareth was divine, the Son of God." A few items later the respondent came across the following:

Suppose that next month a group of archeologists working in the Near East announce the discovery of a group of ancient parchments very similar to the famous Dead Sea Scrolls in a Syrian cave. Radiocarbon dating establishes that the inscriptions were made on parchment between 25 and 50 CE/AD. The language is plainly classical Latin, and the scrolls are quite clearly the "file" that the Romans compiled on Jesus of Nazareth. They establish that Jesus, a carpenter's son of Joseph and Mary from Nazareth, began to preach in present-day Palestine when he was 30, claiming to be the Messiah. Witnesses, including spies sent by the occupying Romans, confirm the miracles reported in the New Testament. Specifically, Jesus turned ordinary water into wine, walked upon water, multiplied loaves and fishes, raised Lazarus to life, and cured scores of people of many serious illnesses. The Roman officials, it is clear from the file, were plainly skeptical of these stories, but painstaking and detailed examination of the evidence could not discredit it and left them very worried and puzzled.

They decided, therefore, to put Jesus to death, fearing he was the Messiah who would overthrow their rule. After the crucifixion, Pontius Pilate made sure Jesus was dead, according to the records, and posted soldiers at the tomb to make sure the body stayed inside. The guards testified that they periodically rolled aside the stone to make sure Jesus' body was exactly as it should be, and the body was unquestionably dead. Then, the guards said, after several days a very bright light suddenly burst from the tomb, the rock fell away, and a very alive and radiant Jesus emerged and spoke to them. The file then contains many reports that Jesus was seen for several weeks thereafter in various parts of Palestine and then disappeared. Pontius Pilate, fearing for his position if the story every reached Rome, ordered the file destroyed and the followers of Jesus persecuted. But instead the file was apparently hidden, then lost until now.

Other scholars examine the scrolls and eventually pronounce them genuine and unaltered in any way. In short, there apparently was a Jesus of Nazareth, and the story of the Gospels is confirmed by records kept by the government at the time.

Now this story is not *true. It is entirely hypothetical. But imagine for the sake of the following question that the discovery* and conclusions *described above actually occurred. How would you* then *respond to the following question, on the -4 to +4 scale you used on the last page?*

____ Jesus of Nazareth was divine, the Son of God.

As you would expect, virtually all of the San Francisco atheists had answered "-4" to that question on the pretest, and 64 percent of them indicated on the posttest that the discovery of such scrolls and their subsequent validation would have absolutely no effect upon their belief. The most common explanations offered were, "This is a ridiculous question," "I don't answer hypothetical questions like this," "This could never happen," "Are you trying to convert us?" "This is the sort of 'miracle' religious people have fabricated in the past," and "Scientific tests can be wrong."

We understand these sentiments; we might react similarly if asked to respond to a hypothetical discovery that surveys are a waste of time. Should such scrolls, once tested and authenticated by the scholarly community, have driven atheists to their knees and forced them to accept Jesus as their personal savior? No. They would establish Jesus' existence, but the stories of miracles and the resurrection could still be discounted. But given how often nonbelievers have cited the paucity of historical records that Jesus ever existed, you would think such scrolls might at least move their -4 to a -3. One big objection would have seemingly been met, and evidence provided for the rest. But about two-thirds of the Bay Area atheists did not budge. Neither did most of the thirty-eight Manitoba parent atheists who got the "nonbeliever booklet" (see note 3 for chapter 1), with 61 percent showing no change or a backlash change.[5]

But wait. We also sent the original, "Jesus never existed" measure home in the believer's booklet answered by forty-five highly fundamentalist parents, which goes as follows:

Suppose that next month a group of archeologists working in the Near East announce the discovery of a group of ancient parchments, very similar to the famous Dead Sea Scrolls, in a Syrian cave. Except these scrolls are somewhat older. Radiocarbon dating establishes that the inscriptions were made on the parchments about 200 B.C. ±100 years. The inscriptions are in ancient Greek and contain many of the myths and teachings of the "mystery religions" which arose in Asia Minor at the time. But what is astounding about these scrolls is that they also contain much of the story of "Jesus" as well.

Specifically, the scrolls tell the story of Attis, a carpenter's son raised in a Greek settlement in what is now Lebanon. Attis was born of a virgin, though in this myth his father was a Zeus-like god. He began a three-year public ministry at the age of thirty, drawing a multitude of followers and eventually coming into conflict with the established religion in his region. Attis was put to death but arose three days later and eventually rose into the heavens. Furthermore, most of the parables, miracle stories, and teachings of the Gospels are found in these scrolls, which clearly predate the reform movement that arose in Judaism during the First Century A.D. and which eventually became Christianity.

Other scholars examine the scrolls and eventually pronounce them genuine and unaltered in any way. Scholars of Near East religions conclude that the long-forgotten myth of Attis was adapted and embellished by a group of Jewish reformers during the Roman occupation of Palestine to suit their own purposes—just as much of the book of Genesis has long been traced to earlier Sumerian myths. In short, there never was a Jesus of Nazareth.

Now this story is not true. It is entirely hypothetical. But imagine for the sake of the following question that the discovery and conclusions described above actually occurred. How would you then respond to the following question, on the -4 to +4 scale you used on the last page?

Ninety-three percent of the fundamentalist parents said this discovery, should it actually occur and be validated as described, would have absolutely no impact on their beliefs. Instead, they explained, "My belief in Jesus does not depend upon such things," "Jesus is Lord," "I would know it was just a trick by Satan," "Jesus died for our sins. Nothing can ever change that," and "That would mean the Bible is false, which cannot possibly be." The near-perfect indifference among these strong believers to evidence that they would be wrong is significantly larger than that found in either atheist sample. But if you think the ancient-scrolls proposition did not tap dogmatism in the case of the atheists, is it fair to say that it did in the case of fundamentalists? Or if you think it did reveal a dogmatic streak in most of the atheists, did it not also capture one in virtually all of these fundamentalists?

WHAT WOULD BE REQUIRED . . . ?

Our second attempt to measure dogmatic behavior involved simply asking the San Francisco atheists the question, "What would be required, what would have to happen, for you to believe in the 'traditional' God described at the beginning of this survey? Are there conceivable events, or evidence, that would lead you to believe? What, for example?"

We got many different answers to this open-ended question. The most common was of the nature, "It would take a clear, undisputable miracle." Others were more demanding: "I'll believe when there is peace on earth and universal brotherhood," and "When a supernatural being appears before me and proves, to *my* satisfaction, that it created everything." Others made supreme demands: "I would believe in a God who could change all the laws of the universe and still make things work," or (whimsically) "If it could explain quantum theory." All of these were counted as positive answers to the question; in fact we accepted almost anything as indicating openness to being shown wrong, including "If I could comb his beard." Nevertheless, 51 percent of the Bay Area atheists said there was nothing conceivable that could change their minds on the existence of the traditional God.

We found this level of closed-mindedness hard to believe, and suspected the wording of our question had not communicated our intention. So we reworked the item for the Alabama/Idaho sample, to make sure the informants knew we would take anything they would consider a test of the matter. Specifically we inserted, "Is there *absolutely nothing* that could happen that would convince you? Or are there *conceivable* events—however unlikely or unprecedented—that would lead you to believe? What?" And 52 percent of the Alabama/Idaho atheists still said nothing could change their minds. Nothing. And the thirty-eight Manitoba parent atheists who encountered this question (in its original wording) were even more locked down, with 57 percent choosing the response, "No, there's nothing."

All of which implies that if the traditional God does exist, an awful lot of atheists are going to miss out on the fact no matter what happens. But suppose this God does not exist. How many fundamentalists are going to believe in it no matter what? We asked forty-five highly fundamentalist parents, "What would be required, what would have to happen, for you to *not* believe in the traditional Judeo-Christian God? That is, are there conceivable events, or evidence, that would lead you to *not* believe?" *All* of them said nothing could do this. They knew, by God! So again as dogmatic as the atheists often were, they were out-dogged by persons who scored very highly on the Religious Fundamentalism scale. For sure, both sides cannot be right. But whoever is wrong appears to be well-inoculated against catching the truth.

SUMMARY

We were surprised by the relatively high DOG scale scores posted by the American atheists, as Canadian nonbelievers had always scored rather low on the measure. Then we were taken aback when most of the Bay Area and Canadian atheists acted dogmatically in the ancient-scrolls experiment. To top it off, a majority in all three atheist samples stated that nothing conceivable could change their minds about the existence of the traditional God. True, the Manitoba fundamentalist parents won every event in the Dogmatism Derby by big margins. But you could hardly say that dogmatism drops with religious belief, or that only true believers are inflexibly wedded to their opinions. Instead it seems you can find high levels of closed-mindedness at each end of the belief spectrum.

Why would people who have railed against the dogmatism of established churches be so rigid in their own beliefs? Taking their point of view, you can see how they might feel entitled to their certainty because, as we saw in the last chapter, most of them once believed in God. "Been there, done that," they could say, and then add, "Saw the flaws, left." They can cite their own history as evidence that they are *not* dogmatic. If they were, they never would have seen the flaws they saw and reacted the way they did. (In contrast, very few theists have ever been atheists, and hence appear more susceptible to the charge of blindly, dogmatically following the path trod by their ancestors.) But does the atheists' present dogmatism feed off their earlier lack of it? Perhaps they have the certainty of their convictions now partly because they have chosen what they believe more than most people have. Could they change their beliefs yet again if these beliefs failed some test? Or would it be harder, precisely because they chose these beliefs? It is one thing to abandon somebody's ideas, which you have simply copied. It is another to find fault in the product of your own thinking.

A second factor that might foster dogmatism in many atheists could be the way scientific discoveries have pushed the traditional God into a tight corner. For starters, the yet-unfathomed vastness of the universe, and the possibility that ours is but one of a huge number of universes, screws Genesis right into the ground. Many atheists may think they have scientific fact at the core of their convictions, so their beliefs *are* justified.

A third factor might lay in the suffering some atheists have endured for their beliefs. If you have paid a significant price for your principles, how comfortable can it be to say, "Well of course I could be wrong"? Having the courage of your convictions may make them extra convincing to you.

Nevertheless the data trouble us. It is one thing to say you have "been there, done that" regarding religion. It is another to say, "The things I believe in are so completely true, I could never doubt them." It is one thing to hold that you are right because science is on your side, but why would you then blow off a scientifically validated finding that shows Jesus actually existed? It is one thing to have suffered for your beliefs, but does that mean nothing conceivable could change your mind about the traditional God?

So, overall, our atheist groups resembled their fundamentalist counterparts much more in dogmatism than we imagined they would. How do you think they'll stack up when it comes to zealotry?

NOTES

1. This study and most of the others described here are reported in chapter 8 of Bob Altemeyer, *The Authoritarian Specter* (Cambridge, MA: Harvard University Press, 1996).

2. See Bob Altemeyer, "Dogmatic Behavior among Students: Testing a New Measure of Dogmatism," *Journal of Social Psychology* 142 (2002): 713–21.

3. The mean DOG score for the Bay Area sample was 87.5 (23.5), that for the Alabama/Idaho group equaled 87.0 (22.6), that of the Manitoba parent atheists was 59.4 (22.6), while the Manitoba fundamentalists had a mean of 124.9 (22.1). Obviously the latter score is significantly larger than all the others, and the Manitoba atheists mean is significantly smaller (beyond the 0.001 level) than either American score. The alpha coefficients for the DOG scale in the three overall samples were 0.85 for the San Francisco atheists, 0.84 for the Alabama/Idaho atheists, and 0.91 for the Manitoba parents.

4. See B. Altemeyer, *Enemies of Freedom* (San Francisco: Jossey-Bass, 1987), pp. 235–37.

5. Four of the thirty-eight atheist parents who got this version of the booklet said the discovery of ancient scrolls supporting Christianity would make them believe even less in Jesus' divinity. You always get *some* goofy things in a batch of surveys, but we suspect this little anomaly was likely due to a "screw you" effect not unknown in pretest/posttest experiments when the participant thinks you are trying to change his mind.

CHAPTER 5

ZEALOTRY

W e made a small joke earlier about the <u>dearth of atheist bumper stickers and Campus Crusades Against Christ</u>. Compared with the zeal with which some religious groups proclaim their beliefs, atheists speak very softly (but carry a big stick in court). As some of the atheists told us in chapter 3, it can cost you a lot if people know you are "against God," and those who advocate atheism on a bumper sticker, or preach nonbelief to neighbors' children the way the neighbors evangelize Christianity to atheists' kids are likely to find themselves in big trouble. As a tiny and (by some) despised minority, atheists could never openly try to convert others the way evangelicals routinely do. What would happen to someone in your town who knocked on people's doors and asked if he could come in and attack the Bible?

But do atheists nevertheless burn with zeal to make their point of view dominant, the way many highly religious people do? They appear to feel strongly about what they do and do not believe. If they dare not go door to door, would they nevertheless try to convert others to atheism if they had the chance? Would they bust a gut to make sure their own children became atheists? Do atheists have a sneaky, secret agenda that says, "First we get rid of prayer in public schools, then we start teaching atheism there instead"? Are they, in short, just as zealous as many fundamentalists, only forced to proselytize in the shadows because of the unpopularity of their beliefs? We gasped at how dogmatic many atheists were. Why wouldn't they then also be zealous, especially those who belong to the active atheists organizations?

We put three measures of missionary zeal in our booklets: "The Questioning Teen," "How Did You Raise Your Own Children?" and "Teaching Atheism in Public Schools." The first two derived from our earlier study of amazing apostates and amazing believers, and the last sprung from research on double standards. In each case we asked, essentially, "How much would you, if you could, shape young people to end up believing what you believe? Or would you instead want young people to make up their own minds about things, without any biasing toward your own point of view?"

1. THE QUESTIONING TEEN

In our 1994–1995 study of amazing converts, we asked both sets of amazing people what they would say to a teenager who came to them for advice about religion.[1] In the case of the apostates, the hypothetical teen had a very religious upbringing but now was starting to question things. Only one of the apostates said he would want the teen to end up like him; instead nearly all indicated they would advise the teen to make a two-sided search of the issue and then decide (or else they said they would offer no advice at all). On the other hand, almost all of the Amazing Believers with a teen parked in front of them who had no religious background, but who now was thinking of becoming more religious, wanted the teen to become a believer like them, and none of them advocated a two-sided search.[2] In short, you could hardly imagine a clearer difference in reactions than we found in these two groups who had traded destinies. At most, only one of the apostates would have proselytized a questioning, searching, and perhaps vulnerable teenager, but almost all of the believers would have.

We set up this situation for our American atheists as follows:

"Suppose a teenager came to you for advice about religion. S/he had been raised a Christian, and religion had played a big part in how s/he had been raised. But now this person is having questions about that religion, and wants your advice on what to do.

    (a)   What would you say?
    (b)   Would you want this person to end up believing what you believe?
    (c)   Would you try to lead them to share your beliefs?"

We had a little difficulty pigeonholing the answers written to the first question, which were occasionally ambiguous. By our count, 62 percent of the San Francisco sample and 63 percent of the Alabama/Idaho atheists would have said something to the troubled teen that would have promoted apostasy (e.g., "I would have told him why I became an atheist," "Religion is ridiculous"). Others might read the answers and say that closer to 50 percent, or 75 percent, would have advocated abandoning religious belief. But most of the active atheists would have thumped the drum for atheism, sometimes softly, sometimes loudly. In contrast, only 8 percent of the Manitoba parent atheists checked an alternative that went, "I'd tell her/him that traditional religious beliefs were, in my opinion, wrong and urge her/him to drop most or all such beliefs." Instead, the vast majority of these parents (86 percent) chose, "I'd tell her/him that s/he should search for alternate religious beliefs, and then decide what s/he wanted to believe." So most of the active American atheists would have said something to the teen that would have promoted apostasy, while almost none of the Manitoba parent atheists would have pushed thataway.

Would the atheists *want* the teen to end up an atheist, either through their influence or through the teen's own search? Most (53 percent) of the Bay Area respondents said yes, as did nearly half (48 percent) of those from Alabama and Idaho. The Manitoba parents followed somewhat behind, at 35 percent.

So would the respondent have deliberately *tried to lead* the teen in this direction? In each sample only a minority said they would: 42 percent of the San Francisco participants, 38 percent of the Alabama/Idaho contingent, and only 16 percent of the Manitoba parent atheists.[3]

How would strong fundamentalists react to a mirror-image situation? We set the scene for the Manitoba parents who scored highly on the Religious Fundamentalism scale as follows:

"Suppose a teenager came to you for advice about religion. S/he had been raised in a nonreligious family as an atheist, but now this person is thinking about becoming much more religious, and wants your advice on what to do."

Nearly all of the fundamentalists (88 percent) said they would tell the teen her parents were wrong and she should become more religious, while only 12 percent said they would advise "search and decide"—neatly flip-flopping the 11 percent versus 86 percent found among the atheist parents. And 96 percent of the highly fundamentalist parents stated they would want this teen to adopt their beliefs, and virtually all (98 percent) revealed they would try to lead the teen in this direction.

So as is shown in figure 5.1, the American atheists showed a moderate level of proselytizing zeal on this "Questioning Teen" measure, the Manitoba parent atheists indicated relatively little, and they all hold a farthing candle to the sun compared to the intense zeal of the fundamentalists.

2. "HOW DID YOU RAISE YOUR OWN CHILDREN?"

In our study of amazing converts, we found that none of the apostates planned to raise his children as nonbelievers. Instead, about half said they would send their kids to church to learn about religion from believers; the others indicated they would let their children learn from others, such as peers, and not bad-mouth whatever religious interest developed. The apostates wanted their children to make up their own minds about religion. In contrast, most (69 percent) of the converted believers told us they would definitely take their children to church and give them the strong religious upbringing they had never received.

These results shaped the question we asked the American atheists in the present study:

"To what extent would you want your children to have the same religious beliefs that you have?" to which we provided the following four possible answers:

(1) I would stress my point of view as they were growing up, trying to get them to adopt my views.

(2) I would want them to make up their own minds, but I would *not* make reli-

Figure 5.1

Responses to "The Questioning Teen" Situation

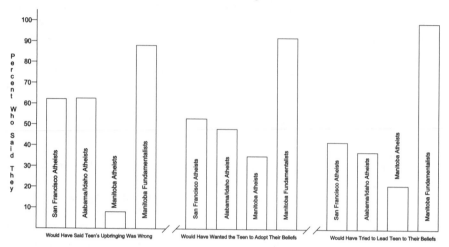

gion an important issue. I would not pressure them to believe as I do, *nor* would I purposely have them exposed to traditional teachings.

(3) I would want them to make up their own minds, and I *would* try to make it an important issue in their lives. I would try to get them to seriously examine many different points of view on religion.

(4) I would see to it they received a strong traditional religious education, and hope they accepted those beliefs.

We also provided space for an "Other" answer for those respondents who could not find their approach in the four listed—but very few respondents used this option.

This hardly constituted a hypothetical question for most of those who responded, persons in their forties, fifties, sixties, and beyond. As some of them wrote in the margins of the questionnaire, they answered according to how they had actually raised their offspring. Only about a fifth (22 percent) of the San Francisco atheists, and 12 percent of the Alabama/Idaho sample checked off the first answer, declaring they had made a determined effort to pass their beliefs onto their children. Instead, most of these active atheists selected either the second option (56 percent in the Bay Area, 44 percent in Alabama/Idaho) or the third (21 percent and 44 percent, respectively). In both cases the parent wanted the child to make up her own mind, with different degrees of emphasis being placed on the matter.

If you bet that some of these atheists would have confessed that they raised their kids in a traditional religion (which you probably did not bet) no one said that. We accordingly gave our Manitoba parents just the first three options. Almost all the atheist parents (86 percent) selected an alternative that went, "I wanted them to make up their own minds, and did not care if they developed different beliefs from mine. But I did *not* make religion an important issue." Only 4 percent chose the option that read, "I wanted them to have the same religious beliefs that I do, and tried to make it an important issue in their lives." In contrast almost all the highly fundamentalist parents (94 percent) affirmed they had made a strong effort to pass their beliefs on to their offspring.

3. TEACHING ATHEISM IN PUBLIC SCHOOLS

Our third measure of proselytizing zeal was rooted in some earlier research on double standards. In 1991 Manitoba students were asked to react to one of two hypothetical situations involving the teaching of religion in public schools. In the first case a law had supposedly been passed requiring the strenuous teaching of Christianity in public schools, aimed at getting the students to eventually accept Jesus Christ as their personal savior. In the second case other students were told of a similar law, except it was set in a modern Arab democracy (where the subject's children went to school), Islam was taught, and the aim was to get the students to become devout Muslims. About half (48 percent) of the students who scored highly on the Right-Wing Authoritarianism scale—a measure that has a high correlation with religious fundamentalism—liked the idea of teaching Christianity in Canadian public schools, but almost none (5 percent) of them thought it would be right for a Muslim state to teach their children Islam in a public school in a Muslim country. In a follow-up study using parents, the numbers came in 40 percent versus 22 percent.

In another follow-up study, most authoritarian students (62 percent) supported Christian indoctrination in Canadian public schools, but only 20 percent supported a parallel stressing of Judaism in Israel if their children were attending school there.

Thus highly authoritarian participants—who are usually religious fundamentalists—more often believed in "majority rights" when they were in the majority, but defended "minority rights" when they were outnumbered. By contrast, in all of these studies persons who scored relatively low on the Right-Wing Authoritarianism scale—who are almost never fundamentalists—opposed any religious indoctrination by any religion in the public schools anywhere. They overwhelmingly and consistently said minority rights should be respected.[4]

These experiments (along with others) appear to reveal a gaping hole in the integrity of high authoritarians. But the less authoritarian nonbelievers were not put to any sort of test, were they, because the issue was always, "Should this religion or that religion be taught in public schools?" What would happen if atheists had the opportunity to endorse a proposal to teach atheism in schools? We took advantage of the present study to find out. Here is the question we asked our three atheist groups:

"Suppose a law were passed requiring strenuous teaching in public schools *against* belief in God and religion. Beginning in kindergarten, all children would be taught that belief in God is unsupported by logic and science, and that traditional religions are based on unreliable scriptures and outdated principles. All children would eventually be encouraged to become atheists or agnostics. How would you react to such a law?" The answers available to them were:

(1) I think this would be a *bad* law. No particular kind of religious beliefs should be taught in public schools.
(2) I think this would be a *good* law. These particular beliefs should be taught in public schools.

A solid majority (78 percent) of the San Francisco atheists said this would be a bad law; the figure was 68 percent in Alabama/Idaho. *All* of the Manitoba parent atheists reacted *against* this law.

We also presented the Manitoba parent fundamentalists with the corresponding proposition:

"Suppose a law were passed requiring the strenuous teaching of religion in public schools. Beginning in kindergarten, all children would be taught to believe in God, pray together in school several times each day, memorize the Ten Commandments and other parts of the Bible, learn the principles of Christian morality, and eventually be encouraged to accept Jesus Christ as their personal savior.

How would you react to such a law?"

A solid 84 percent of the fundamentalist parents liked this notion, saying this would be a good law. Figure 5.2 displays these results, as well as those for the child-rearing study described earlier.

If we can assume that atheists would oppose a law promoting Christianity, and that fundamentalists would detest a law inculcating atheism—about as safe an assumption as you can make in this business—then the atheists come out of this study looking pretty good, and the fundamentalists look pretty hypocritical. Most atheists seem to abide by the principle, often stated by atheist groups, that no particular religious outlook should be taught in public schools. That apparently includes their own. Our high fundamentalists, on the other hand, would certainly think it unfair and wrong to have atheism imposed on their children in such schools, but they would approve the forced teaching of their own views to everybody else's children. That hardly seems in keeping with the Golden Rule.

DISCUSSION

So, how zealous do atheists appear to be? Most of the active American atheists would have promoted their own beliefs to a questioning teen, and wanted the teen to adopt their beliefs. Most of the Manitoba parent atheists would not have. But a large majority in all three atheist samples said they did not raise their children in their beliefs, but instead wanted their kids to make up their own minds. And relatively few

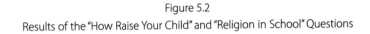

Figure 5.2

Results of the "How Raise Your Child" and "Religion in School" Questions

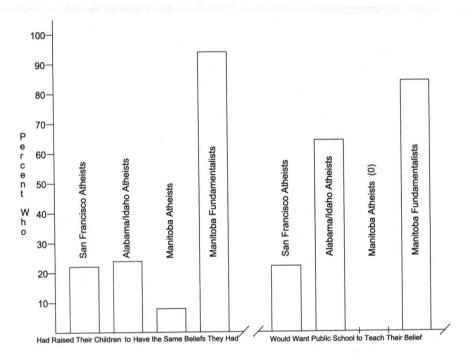

of them approved of teaching atheism in public schools. So all in all, these folks would make poor recruiting sergeants for the Atheist Armed Forces. Certainly they seem like pikers compared with the enormous zeal of the Manitoba fundamentalists, who would have promoted their beliefs to a questioning teen, wanted the teen to join their flock, and would have tried to lead her there, just as they tried to bring up their own children in the fold and keep them there, just as they embraced a law requiring the teaching of their religious beliefs in public schools.

Given how dogmatic the atheists appeared to be, why are they not more zealous? Why especially would they not raise their children to believe what they believe, something that is widely acknowledged to be a basic right of parents? Perhaps they felt they did not have to preach disbelief, or deride faith, for their own children to end up atheists. They may have believed "You've got to be taught" to believe in God to end up a theist. Thus if they did nothing, their offspring would probably end up nonbelievers when all the societal influences had run their course. So maybe they just played it cool.

But the atheists also indicated they would not mind if their children ended up believing in God. First and foremost, they wanted their progeny to make up their own minds. This would also explain why they would not want the enormous help of having the school system propagandize their views: people should not be forced to believe, not be indoctrinated in any system of religious beliefs. This sentiment, you will recall, was also strongly espoused by our Amazing Apostates in 1994–1995.

Is it hard to believe atheists would highly value the individual making up her own mind? After all, as we saw in chapter 3, most of them were themselves once religious and they decided for themselves. Would they deny others that privilege? Even in the case of the questioning teen, while most atheists would have said something that promoted nonbelief, most of them also indicated they would not have tried to lead the teen to their beliefs—compared with the solid majority of Manitoba fundamentalists who would have unhesitatingly sallied forth to bring the teen into their church.

So it seems that these nonbelievers are, by and large, highly principled persons. Some readers might have difficulty believing that of "godless atheists." But these same people would probably have been surprised by the finding in the public-school experiment that atheists answered with much greater integrity than strong fundamentalists did.

Perhaps we are asking the wrong question here. Why are fundamentalists so evangelical? Why have they adopted *this* missionary position with such vigor? Beyond the obvious answers, e.g., preaching the "Good News" has been part of Christianity from the beginning and is especially promoted in certain denominations, devout Christians would probably say they are trying to do the unconverted a huge favor: to bring to them the joy they themselves experience in Jesus, to furnish eternal answers in a world of doubt, to share the peace they have found, to embrace them in the fellowship of the church, to provide salvation for their immortal souls and help them enter heaven for all eternity. In the case of their own children, they would likely say they have a sacred *duty* to bring the issue God has given them to Christ. If their offshoots make their own choices, they might choose wrongly and shoot off badly. What could be more important than serving God? What could be worse than serving Satan? So, it seems that strong fundamentalists proselytize because of the intensity of their beliefs. The fire comes from within. They personally know Jesus, they believe.

But fundamentalists also appear to believe, "You've got to be taught" to end up a theist. Does it work? No and yes and no. As we saw in the introduction, the number of Americans who call themselves religious fundamentalists peaked at 36 percent in 1987, and has since dropped to 30 percent. In Canada, the percentage of "conservative" Protestants has remained at about 8 percent for decades. In our Manitoba studies over the past ten years, in which we compared parents' present religion with their home religion, the fundamentalists had increased their flock by 18 percent over their starting point by converting discontented Catholics, Anglicans, Lutherans, and so on. But at least in our samples, the fundamentalists had to proselytize to survive, because they had one of the worst retention records of any religious group. Barely half (56 percent) of the parents who were raised in a fundamentalist faith were still in such churches by age forty-something.[5] Even those who are emphatically "taught" wander away to a remarkable extent.

These "lost sheep" told us they sometimes left their home religion because the believers in their church were so hostile toward those in other churches. How religiously ethnocentric do you suppose atheists might be?

NOTES

1. See Bob Altemeyer and Bruce Hunsberger, *Amazing Conversions: Why Some Turn to Faith and Others Abandon Religion* (Amherst, NY: Prometheus Books, 1997), pp. 121–22 and 203–204.

2. We try to see things from the perspective of our participants, as well as from a broader viewpoint. Thus we wrote in *Amazing Conversions*, page 218, "Suppose you had discovered the perfect way to live life, a way that solved all your problems and promised you an eternity of happiness. Would it not be selfish to keep the news to yourself? One can argue whether the Amazing Believers have actually discovered what they think they have, just as one can debate whether the Amazing Apostates did the right thing. But given the Believers' backgrounds, it must certainly seem to them that they have found the key to life. And so they would send the seeker on a one-sided search."

3. How do we square these low "I would have tried" numbers to our higher "They would have said something that promoted apostasy"? Some of the atheists wrote something like, "I'd have told him why I am an atheist," which we called a promotion of atheism, but which they might see as just giving information, with no intent to persuade.

4. See B. Altemeyer, *The Authoritarian Specter* (Cambridge, MA: Harvard University Press, 1996), pp. 115–17.

5. See B. Altemeyer, "The Decline of Organized Religion in Western Civilization," *International Journal for the Psychology of Religion* 14 (2004): 77–89.

CHAPTER 6

RELIGIOUS ETHNOCENTRISM

Ethnocentrism means splitting the world into in-groups and out-groups—something most of us do rather automatically. In fact research has shown that even youngsters tend to favor those in "their group" more than they do peers who belong to other groups. Even when schoolchildren knew their class had been divided into two groups at random and no one knew who was in which group, they liked whatever group they now supposedly belonged to better.[1] So if you have ever watched a cowboys and Indians movie told from the cowboys' perspective, and rooted for the cowboys, but instead found yourself cheering for the indigenous people when the movie took their point of view, this may be part of the reason why. When we identify with a group, we usually like it more, and other groups less. Much racial and ethnic prejudice flows from this simple reaction.

The ethnocentric heart beats stronger in some people than in others, however. Religious fundamentalists, for example, tend to be a little more racially prejudiced than most folks, which would undoubtedly surprise them.[2] Partly this happens because fundamentalists tend to be less educated than most people, and education (modestly) lowers prejudice. But fundamentalists' prejudice has other roots as well, as we shall see. One explanation says that the religious training that fundamentalists tend to get as young children, which stresses that they and their co-believers belong to *the* true religion and everybody else does not, creates a template for in-group versus out-group distinctions that greases the skids for racial discrimination later.[3]

If this is true, one might predict that religious fundamentalists will—compared with most people—dislike other religions, which they may have been taught to dislike since early childhood and which their in-group may continue to lambaste. This prediction might seem precarious because devout members of different religions actually have a lot in common, compared with the less pious unwashed masses, and that should attract them to one another. However, important differences would quickly arise, and devout members of various religions have a history of settling these differences with swords and bonfires, and now car bombs. So perhaps the prediction will not come a cropper.

Exhibit 6.1
The Religious Ethnocentrism Scale

____ 1. Christian prayer (and only Christian prayer) should be said in our public schools.

____ 2. I would *not* mind if my child had atheist teachers in elementary school.

____ 3. Our country should always be a Christian country, and other beliefs should be ignored in our public institutions.

____ 4. If there is a heaven, good people will go to it no matter what religion they belong to, if any.

____ 5. If an acquaintance invited me to her temple to see a ceremony such as a Bar Mitzvah or Jewish evening prayers, I would have no religious hesitation about going.

____ 6. I am appalled that tax dollars go to public television when they feature programs on evolution, pagan religions, and other un-Christian topics.

____ 7. You can trust members of all religions equally; no one religion produces better people than any other does.

____ 8. Non-Christian religions have a lot of weird beliefs and pagan ways that Christians should avoid having any contact with.

____ 9. All people may be entitled to their own religious beliefs, but I don't want to associate with people whose views are quite different from my own.

____ 10. People who belong to different religions are probably just as nice and moral as those who belong to mine.

____ 11. If a politician were an atheist, I would refuse to vote for him even if I agreed with all his other ideas.

____ 12. I would like my church to hold joint services with a wide variety of other religions.

____ 13. I would *not* mind at all if my son's best friends were all atheists.

____ 14. I would be against letting some other, different religion use my church for its services when we were not using it.

____ 15. If it were possible, I'd rather have a job where I worked with people with the same religious views I have rather than with people with different views.

____ 16. It would *not* bother me if my children regularly went to some other religion's "youth group" with their friends.

Note: Responses are scored as follows: For Items 1, 3, 6, 8, 9, 11, 14, and 15, a -4 is coded as 1, a -3 is coded as 2, a -2 is coded as 3, a -1 is coded as 4, a 0 is coded as 5, a +1 is coded as 6, a +2 is coded as 7, a +3 is coded as 8, and a +4 is coded as 9. For the other items, the scoring key is reversed. That is, -4 is coded as 9; -3 is coded as 8, and so on up to +4 being coded as 1.

THE RELIGIOUS ETHNOCENTRISM SCALE

We measure religious ethnocentrism with a sixteen-item scale bearing that name. You are once again invited to respond to its statements, shown in table 6.1, on the ever-popular -4 to +4 basis. Note that some of the items mention Christian practice and belief, so the instrument measures religious ethnocentrism among Christians better than it would among, say, Muslims. Note also that you know what the scale measures, so don't be too delighted if you turn out to be magnificently broad-minded.

Scores on the scale could register as low as 16 or as high as 144, with 80 being the halfway point. In the 2002 parent study that supplied our Manitoba atheists and high fundamentalists, 575 parents indicated they presently identified with some Christian religion. Their Religious Ethnocentrism scores ranged from that lowest possible 16 to a dramatically ethnocentric 127. The middle person in the distribution scored a 59, indicating the Manitoba Christian parents as a whole tended *not* to be religiously ethnocentric. But the fifty-one highly fundamentalist parents saturated the upper range, with scores running from 58 to that 127, and a median of 102.

Interestingly, "other religions" tended to get lumped with atheists in the minds of high scorers on this measure. You can tell this by looking at how the answers to one item correlate with the answers to other statements. Three of the items (nos. 2, 11, and 13) specifically mention atheists, and to be sure they drew relatively ethnocentric responses from those 575 Christian parents. But each of those "atheist" items had a *positive* correlation with every one of the other items on the scale. What does that mean? It means the people were not thinking, "Atheists, bad; Jews, Muslims, Hindus, etc. good," but "Atheists, bad; other religions, certainly not good." A religion different from their own belonged to an out-group, especially among the highly fundamentalist parents, who drew the sharpest distinctions.[4]

How did the fifty-one parent atheists do on this instrument, if you don't mind a silly question? Their scores ranged from 16 to 68 and had a median of 38. But of course they would score low on a measure of Christian religious ethnocentrism. How would atheists do on a test of *atheist* religious ethnocentrism? Do they also draw sharp lines between their nonreligious in-group and everyone else?

We devised such a measure for our American atheist samples by adapting six items from the Religious Ethnocentrism scale which read:

____ I would not mind if my child had devoutly religious teachers in elementary school.
____ All people may be entitled to their own religious beliefs, but I don't want to associate with people whose views are quite different from my own.
____ I would not mind at all if my son's best friends were all highly religious.
____ If a politician were deeply religious, I would refuse to vote for him even if I agreed with all his other ideas.
____ It would not bother me if my children regularly went to some religion's "youth group" with their friends.
____ If it were possible, I'd rather have a job where I worked with people with the same views about religion that I have, rather than with people with different views.

Answered on the -4 to +4 basis, summed scores in the San Francisco sample ran the gamut from the minimalist 6 to 54, the highest level of atheist ethnocentrism possible. The median equaled 33. Their Alabama/Idaho counterparts clustered together more, with scores ranging from 18 to 45, and a median of 27. The two American samples gave similar responses to five of the six items. But on the first, the Bay Area participants greatly disliked the idea of their children having a devoutly religious teacher in elementary school (their median answer was -3), while the Alabama/Idaho atheists had a median of +2. (One suspects the latter group had encountered more devout teachers in their children's schools, and was not as bothered by the idea.)

The Manitoba parents only answered the original sixteen-item Religious Ethnocentrism scale, so we do not have scores from the Manitoba atheists on the six-item "atheist version" of the measure. But we can compute a score for the Manitoba fundamentalists over the six original items from the Christian measure. Those computations produced scores that ran from 15 to 49 with a median of 39. The fundamentalists reacted especially against the idea of an atheist teaching their children, and their son having atheists as best friends (medians of -3s in each case).[5]

MEASURING PREJUDICE WITH A THERMOMETER

Did it occur to you, as you were reading this last section, that at least some of our respondents would have figured out that we were trying to measure religious prejudice? If this happened, the results *could* have been infected by a scurvy survey disease called the social desirability effect, whereby people present positive but untrue pictures of themselves. Whether the responses were or were not so afflicted in this case, you ain't seen nothin' yet when it comes to blatant measures of prejudice.

Say, what do you think of Jews in general? How about Muslims, as a group? What about New Yorkers, taken altogether? "What stupid questions!" you might well react. The individuals who make up these broad groups differ so enormously among themselves, one cannot possibly, fairly make such blanket evaluations. "In general," "as a group," and "taken altogether" become inoperable concepts in this context, and they invite the worst kind of overgeneralization—worse even than the ones social scientists make. Few people, certainly few educated people, would deign give an answer to such questions, right?

Ding dong, we're wrong. The damned thing is, if you ask individuals to evaluate some group-in-general, while giving them a way to say "Buzz off" (or possibly something more colorful), most people give you an evaluation. It no doubt helps if the respondents are answering anonymously. But like it or not, people appear to think in such terms—and for an understandable reason. Generalizing helps us handle the otherwise un-handleable, enormous detail in life. The trouble is, we don't know when to stop doing it.

Exhibit 6.2 reproduces a second measure of religious ethnocentrism that we included in our surveys, called "Thermometer." It's offensive, isn't it? Now put yourself in the shoes of a respondent. You don't have to answer the question, and if you do answer, nothing will happen to you no matter what you mark down. Can you not see several simple ways to say "Buzz off" to Thermometer? You could simply skip the question. Or you could put down the same answer (such as "50") for each group as your way of saying, "I judge people as individuals, not as members of a religious or ethnic group."

Of the 253 Bay Area atheists, ten declined to give any answers to Thermometer and one person gave all the categories a rating of 100. Among the twenty-eight Alabama/Idaho atheists, one did not answer and another gave all 50s. All of the fifty-

---

Exhibit 6.2
The "Thermometer Measure" of Religious Ethnocentrism

Please rate your *overall attitude toward* the groups below, using the "evaluation thermometer" printed to the right. If you have a favorable attitude toward a specific group, you would indicate a score somewhere between 50 degrees and 100 degrees, depending on how favorable your evaluation is of that group. On the other hand, if you have an *un*favorable attitude toward a specific group, you could give them a score somewhere between 0 degrees and 50 degrees, depending on how *un*favorable your evaluation is of that group. The labels provided will help you to locate your rating on the thermometer. However, you are *not* restricted to the numbers indicated—feel free to use any number between 0 degrees and 100 degrees.

100	Extremely favorable
90	Very favorable
80	Quite favorable
70	Fairly favorable
60	Slightly favorable
50	Neither favorable
	nor unfavorable
40	Slightly unfavorable
30	Fairly unfavorable
20	Quite unfavorable
10	Very unfavorable
0	Extremely unfavorable

1. ____ Christians
2. ____ Christian fundamentalists
3. ____ People who believe in a "traditional" God
4. ____ Atheists
5. ____ Hindus
6. ____ People who are not sure, one way or the other, whether the "traditional" God exists
7. ____ Jews
8. ____ Jewish fundamentalists
9. ____ Muslims
10. ____ Muslim fundamentalists

one Manitoba parent atheists answered, but eight of them gave all categories a 50. All of the forty-seven Manitoba fundamentalist parents who are Christians answered, with one of them giving all 80s. Summing it up, of the 379 persons involved, 361 (95 percent) obliged us researchers and gave different ratings to some of the groups targeted—even though that potentially made them, the respondents, look prejudiced. Sometimes they skipped a group or two, but in the vast majority of cases our participants rated all ten groups, usually with a wide range of evaluations.

So who likes whom? The San Francisco atheists gave their highest rating to (Surprise!) "Atheists"—with the median being 90. Whom did they like the least? Any kind of fundamentalist: Christian (median = 10), Jewish (median = 10), and Muslim (median = 0). That's some kind of point spread. A huge pit yawns between these atheists' evaluations of their in-group and those out-groups.[6]

The Alabama/Idaho atheists responded similarly, with "Atheists" having a median score of 90. Except in their case the median for all three fundamentalist groups equaled zero, meaning most of them flat-out gave a zero to any kind of fundamentalist. So their division rent even wider, virtually to the max.

In contrast, the Manitoba parent atheists discriminated very little between "Atheists" (median = 50) and any fundamentalist (30 for Christian, 40 for Jewish, and 30 for Muslim). As symbolized by the eight in their ranks who gave every group a rating of 50, these atheists almost flat-lined their evaluations. They viewed all religions virtually the same, and virtually the same as themselves.

The Manitoba parent fundamentalists[7] gave both "Christians" and "People who believe in a 'traditional' God" median ratings of 90. "Christian fundamentalists" had a median of 80. (Although these parents scored very highly on the Religious Fundamentalism scale, some of them [e.g., the Catholics] do not necessarily see themselves as "Christian fundamentalists," and many Protestants shun the label now.) They gave their lowest rating to "Atheists," with the median being 30. So their biggest in-group versus out-group gap equaled $(90 - 30 =) 60$, that of the Manitoba atheist parents equaled $(50 - 30 =) 20$, but those of the Bay Area and Alabama/Idaho atheists came in with a thud at 80 and 90 respectively. See table 6.1.[8]

DISCUSSION

The atheist and fundamentalist groups who answered the six-item religious ethnocentrism measures we pitched their ways showed roughly the same degree of in-group versus out-group discrimination, although the Manitoba fundamentalists once again topped the charts. But when it came to blatantly saying how much they liked various religious groups, the American atheists revealed a huge favoritism for their own kind and an equally massive dislike of fundamentalists. (See figure 6.1.) The Manitoba atheists showed the least bias of our four groups, and this time the Manitoba fundamentalists had to settle for third place. (Sketching in the latter's median of 90 for "Christians" in figure 6.1 does not really change anything, does it?)

Table 6.1
Medians of Ratings of Various Religious Groups by the
Samples in This Study on 0–100 Scale

Target Group	San Francisco Atheists	Alabama/ Idaho Atheists	Manitoba Parent Atheists	Manitoba Parent Fundamentalists
Christians	40	40	50	90
Christian Fundamentalists	10	0	30	80
Believe in a "Traditional" God	40	40	50	90
Atheists	90	90	50	30
Hindus	50	50	50	50
Not Sure One Way or the Other	70	60	50	50
Jews	50	50	50	50
Jewish Fundamentalists	10	0	40	50
Muslims	40	40	50	50
Muslim Fundamentalists	0	0	30	50

Note: The median is the score in the middle of a distribution of scores.

The essence of prejudice, both as a word and as a thought, involves prejudging. It most commonly involves assessing someone on the basis of groups she belongs to, rather than on who she is, how she acts. How much we do this probably depends on—among other things—how big a distinction we make between our in-groups and all the out-groups we don't like as much. Looking at figure 6.1, it certainly appears that the active American atheists are very ethnocentric religiously. Again, because of our prior experience with Canadian atheists, this came as a thunderclap. We especially expected the Bay Area atheists to be much less ethnocentric. It probably surprises them, too.

Then why is it so? Putting ourselves inside the active atheists' minds, we realize that many of them have personally suffered from attacks by Christian fundamental-

Figure 6.1

Results of the Two Religious Ethnocentrism Surveys

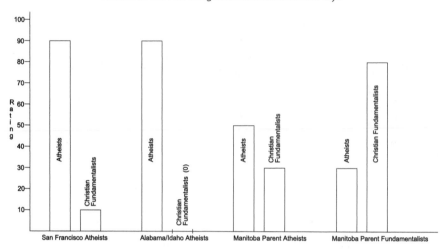

ists. They might well prefer to associate with, and to work with people who share their own religious views because they might otherwise pay a price for their atheism. As well, fundamentalists have been their chief opponents in court, and their major enemies as they try to send their children to public schools where their kids will not be indoctrinated in Christianity, be taught "creation science," and so on. Atheists are probably turned off big-time by fundamentalists' proselytizing and their positions on many social issues. And, of course, fundamentalists vociferously condemn atheists, whom they see as a major corrupting threat to the American way of life. Does anybody remember that Communism was usually described as "atheistic Communism" and even the double damn of "Godless atheistic Communism"?

These would comprise a good enough explanation except for the fact that our two American atheist groups also bad-mouthed Jewish and Muslim fundamentalists. Few atheists have probably had personal run-ins with these groups. Zealous rabbis and mullahs haven't been advocating school prayer, haven't been loudly condemning the theory of evolution, haven't been shaping social policy legislation, and so on. Yet the active American atheists loathe them as much or more than they do the Christian fundamentalists, with median ratings of "extremely unfavorable" and "very unfavorable." While some of this probably reflects fundamentalists' activity in other countries, you have to suspect that much of this blanket rejection arises because any brand of religious fundamentalism disagrees so completely with atheism.

Social psychologists had little trouble experimentally confirming decades ago that birds of a feather flock together, that people who agree about things tend to like each other. And on the other hand . . . So if a group holds down the anchor point at one end of a continuum of beliefs, as atheists do regarding the existence of God and the value of religion, whom are they likely to dislike the most? The folks at the other end of the spectrum—religious fundamentalists. This reaction does not always occur with explosive force: Manitoba parent atheists did not reject fundamentalists all that much, *nor* did their fundamentalist counterparts bash atheists to the nth degree. But perhaps Canada has a stronger tradition of tolerance, and opinions about religion have not been polarized there as they have been in the cauldron of American elections, legislatures, and Supreme Court cases.

If American fundamentalists are very ethnocentric religiously (and remember, we have no data on American fundamentalists), they would seemingly be matched by the ethnocentrism of some active atheists in their country. It does not have to be this way, but both sides may feel it a very natural reaction. Can both sides also agree it is very unfortunate?

NOTES

1. See the research on the "minimal group effect" in H. Tajfel, ed., *Differentiation between Social Groups* (New York: Academic Press, 1978).

2. See Bob Altemeyer and Bruce Hunsberger, "Authoritarianism, Religious Fundamentalism, Quest and Prejudice," *International Journal for the Psychology of Religion* 2 (1992): 113–33.

3. See Bob Altemeyer, "Why Do Religious Fundamentalists Tend to Be Prejudiced?" *International Journal for the Psychology of Religion* 13 (2003): 17–28.

4. The mean inter-item correlation for the sixteen items equaled 0.297 for these 575 Christian respondents, yielding an alpha coefficient of 0.872. For the whole sample of 836, the respective values were 0.295 and 0.870.

5. This is an occasion where statistical significance is not obvious at a glance. The *mean* of the six-item sum for the San Francisco atheists was 32.8 (sd = 8.93), that for the Alabama/Idaho atheists equaled 27.04 (6.02), and that for the Manitoba fundamentalist parents on the six corresponding items was 37.96 (7.45). The latter score was significantly higher than either American atheist mean at beyond the 0.0001 level (t = 4.37 for the Bay Area comparison, and 4.40 for the Alabama/Idaho scores).

6. We added "Buddhists" to the list given the Alabama/Idaho atheists, and it pulled a median rating of 50. We also added an exploratory concept, "'Fundamentalist' atheists." We provided a place for the respondent to indicate "This last one does not exist," and eight of the twenty-eight atheists checked it. But the other respondents apparently think such people exist, and gave them ratings whose median was 40—certainly higher than those that the Christian, Jewish, and Muslim fundamentalists got, but lower than the 90 accorded ordinary atheists.

7. For this analysis we have dropped the four Muslim parents who scored very highly on the Religious Fundamentalism scale.

8. Want some means? Here are the critical ones for the comparisons we suspect most people will want to make, with standard deviations in parentheses. Bay Area—Christian Fundamentalists: 11.5 (15.9); Atheists: 84.2 (16.4). Difference: 72.7 (25.2). Alabama/Idaho atheists—Christian Fundamentalists: 7.0 (12.3); Atheists: 84.6 (17.3); Difference: 77.6 (25.1). Manitoba Parent Atheists—Christian Fundamentalists: 30.2 (20.2); Atheists: 61.0 (16.3); Difference: 30.8 (30.1). Manitoba Parent Fundamentalists—Christians: 93.3 (6.3); Christian

Fundamentalists 80.4 (18.3); People who believe in a traditional God: 87.7 (11.1); Atheists: 28.3 (26.9). Biggest difference: 65.0 (27.3) between Christians and Atheists. Difference between Christian Fundamentalists and Atheists: 52.1 (29.5).

Want some tests of statistical significance? Using a t-test for differences between means when the means themselves are differences based on the same individuals in each group, and assuming the population variances are not equal, and considering the sample sizes as "large," and not partitioning alpha, then: (A) The biggest Manitoba Parent atheist "gap" is significantly *smaller* than any other group's biggest gap. But you knew that already, right? (B) The San Francisco gap between "Christian Fundamentalists" and "Atheists" (72.7) is *not* significantly larger than the Manitoba parent fundamentalist's biggest gap of 65.0 ("Christians" vs. "Atheists") by a two-tailed test: $t = 1.77$, $p > 0.05$. (C) It is, however, significantly larger than the Manitoba parent fundamentalist's mirror-image ("Christian Fundamentalists" vs. "Atheists") gap of 52.1: $t = 4.44$; $p < 0.001$ no matter how many tails the test has.

CHAPTER 7

OTHER FINDINGS

A ren't you colossally impressed at how well the authors of this book have predicted the results of this study? We were sure the American atheists would score low on dogmatism, but they came in rather high. Given their high marks in dogmatism, we figured they would be rather zealous, but we were proved wrong. Then we believed these atheists would score low in religious ethnocentrism, and instead the data blew us away. You might well wonder why you are reading this book, given what dunderheads its authors have turned out to be. But we are beholding here the great advantage of scientific investigation: it tells you when you are wrong. And Mother Nature has been particularly forthcoming in this regard in the last three chapters. So read on. We may not have a clue about what the heck's going on, but we shall find out.

This chapter closes the book on the American survey by discussing two questions not yet treated. Then we shall present findings about sundry topics raised only in the Manitoba study. These will produce a minor mystery, which we shall try to solve at chapter's end. The solution will lead to a host of predictions about American atheists in general in the next chapter—predictions that we hope will fare better than those reviewed above.

HAPPINESS, JOY, AND COMFORT FROM SCIENCE

In 1996 we asked over five hundred Manitoba parents, "To what extent do traditional religious beliefs bring you *happiness, joy, and comfort?*" We suggested sixteen different ways it might, such as "They tell me the purpose of my life," "They help me deal with personal pain and suffering," and "They make me feel safe in the protection of God." Each item was answered on a 0 to 6 basis, so summed scores could range from 0 to 96 with 48 being the midpoint. The average response of the parents equaled 53. We also gave them sixteen ways in which logic and science might bring them happiness, joy, and comfort. Eight of these were identical to those on the "Religion makes me happy" version, but the rest were tailored to benefits that science presumably brings big-time, benefits we personally have experienced recently such as "They serve as a check on my own biases and wrong ideas." However, the sixteen "logic and science" items spawned much smaller payouts to the parents, with the median being only 33.[1]

Not surprisingly, persons who scored high on the Religious Fundamentalism scale reported getting the greatest comfort and joy from religion, and the least from logic and science. If we muster the fifty-one parents who scored highest in fundamentalism back then, they had a median of 82 on the "religion brings happiness" scale (an average of over 5 per item on the 0 to 6 response scale used) and a median of 12 on the "science brings happiness" measure (an average of less than 1). We could not find any subsample among the parents who gushed about logic and science the way the fundamentalists acclaimed religion.

Well, maybe a batch of confirmed, active atheists would. So we packed the "science brings happiness" items, shown in exhibit 7.1, toward the end of the booklet sent to the San Francisco sample. We found that, indeed, logic and science did bring much more happiness, joy, and comfort to this well-educated, logic-lauding, science-citing set than it did to our Manitoba parents. But the Bay Area median of 56 could not compare to the happiness that religion brought to high fundamentalists. Only a few proposed rewards drew the kind of raves that fundamentalists gave religion. The atheists had medians of 6 for, "They provide the surest path we have to the truth," "They enable me to search for the truth, instead of just memorizing what others say," and "They give the satisfaction of knowing that my beliefs are based upon objective facts and logic, not an act of faith." Only numbers 4, 8, and 14 had medians of 5. In contrast, *all* of the sixteen "religion brings happiness" items had medians of 5 or 6 among the fundamentalists.

Of course, logic and science are not intended to take away fear of death or control evil impulses, so the comparison reeks with unfairness. But even if we discount the religion-favored items in exhibit 7.1, we still struggle to find benefits of logic and science among these active atheists that match the personal happiness religion brings to its true believers. *Should* we expect such cerebral activities to provide big-bang emotional payoffs? No, 'tis also unfair. But big-bang emotional payoffs satisfy important human needs that logic and science cannot, and ignoring that "would seem illogical, Captain." If someone is puzzled why so many people invest in religion, how puzzling is it, really? Is it not more impressive that increasing numbers of people can do without it? After all, nonbelievers are taking a pass on some of the most emotionally satisfying experiences in life, it would seem. Perhaps even believers can agree, "That takes guts."

Exhibit 7.1
The "Science Brings Happiness" Scale Sent to the San Francisco Atheists

Some people cannot accept traditional religious teachings because they require an act of faith. They base their beliefs instead on logic and science. Would you now indicate to what extent *logic and science* bring you **happiness, joy, and comfort** in each of the following ways?

0 = To no extent at all   3 = To a moderate extent   6 = To a great extent
1 = To a slight extent   4 = To an appreciable extent
2 = To a mild extent   5 = To a considerable extent

_____   1. They tell me the purpose of my life. (How much happiness, joy, and comfort have logic and science given you through their explanation of the purpose of your life?)
_____   2. They provide the surest path we have to the truth.
_____   3. They help me deal with personal pain and suffering.
_____   4. They enable me to work out my own beliefs and philosophy of life.
_____   5. They take away fear of dying.
_____   6. They enable me to search for the truth, instead of just memorizing what others say.
_____   7. They tell me what is right and wrong.
_____   8. They serve as a check on my own biases and wrong ideas.
_____   9. They provide an anchor in my life that keeps me from going astray.
_____   10. They explain the mysteries of life.
_____   11. They help me control evil impulses.
_____   12. They have provided satisfying answers to all the questions in life.
_____   13. They make me feel safe.
_____   14. They bring me the joy of discovery.
_____   15. They reveal how I can live a happy life.
_____   16. They give me the satisfaction of knowing that my beliefs are based upon objective fact and logic, not an act of faith.

THE "HIDDEN OBSERVER"

We once asked over four hundred Manitoba university students if they had doubts that they were created by an Almighty God who will judge each person and take some into heaven for eternity while casting others into hell forever. Except we did not exactly ask "them" to respond. Instead we drew upon an innovation in hypnosis research and posed the question to their "Hidden Observer." What's that? A "hypnotized" person with her arm in ice water will usually insist her arm feels fine if the hypnotist tells her it does, but she might also make a gesture (suggested by the hypnotist) if her arm does hurt. That ability to betray public utterances is attributed to a metaphorical Hidden Observer. Thus, we asked the students to stand aside, as it were, and let their Hidden Observers indicate if they had significant doubts about the traditional God. *One third* of the highly authoritarian students checked off, "Yes, (s)he has secret doubts which (s)he has kept strictly to herself/himself that this really is true." That's a lot of supposedly strong theists harboring secret doubts.

We wondered if the same might not also be true among active atheists. After all, an atheist is staring into the void with no God to go to for help, no confessional, no afterlife, and all around him are people saying he's missed the most obvious fact of existence. Why has he bet against Pascal's wager, supposedly "a sure thing"? Would all this not understandably stir up some second-guessing?

Accordingly we raised the issue with a "hard question" toward the end of the Bay Area booklet as follows:

> Imagine for the sake of argument that you have a "Hidden Observer" in you, which knows your every thought and deed, but which only speaks when it is safe to do so, and when directly spoken to. This question is for your Hidden Observer. "Does this person (that is, you) have *doubts about her/his 'public' stand* on the existence of God? Does this person actually believe that the traditional God of Judeo-Christian religions really exists?"
>
> Yes (s)he has secret doubts about her/his "public" stand on the existence of God, which (s)he has kept strictly to herself/himself.
>
> Yes, (s)he has doubts about her/his "public stand," but others (such as parents or friends) know (s)he has these doubts.
>
> No, (s)he totally believes her/his "public" stand.
>
> Other: _____

Of the 253 respondents in the San Francisco sample, 236 answered this question. (Some of the decliners wrote that the question betrayed our supposed secret agenda: e.g., "This is another attempt to get us to believe in God, isn't it!") Of those 236, only 9 (4 percent) checked off the "secret doubts" option. Instead, the vast majority (218, or 92 percent) declared, "No, (s)he totally believes her/his 'public' stand."

Perhaps this sheds some light on the dogmatism finding. Some people seem to be dogmatic out of desperation. They discover, through arguments with others and through their own ruminations, that they cannot adequately explain their beliefs. So they opt for a "no-brainer" defense, simply to obstinately insist all their beliefs must be true. This "circle the wagons" defensive dogmatism may especially appear in people who belong to a religion because of strong social pressure. They may have their doubts, but these could never be publicly admitted. Only a hidden observer might spill the beans.

But atheists can usually tell you, in chapter and verse, why they do not believe. And how many atheists deny God's existence because of social pressure? They have chosen, as we saw in chapter 3, to believe not. So, whatever their reasons for being dogmatic, our atheists do not appear locked down because in their heart of hearts they fear they are wrong. They seem to truly believe what they do not believe.

MANITOBA PARENT STUDIES

Evolution versus Creation Science

Here's an easy one, with only a small surprise. The 2002 parent study that provided our Manitoba atheists and high fundamentalists included in its booklet a twelve-item

---

Exhibit 7.2
The Evolution versus Creation Science Scale

1. Darwin's theory of evolution says that human beings descended from monkeys.
2. Evolution is *not* "just a theory," but a scientifically established fact now.
3. Life on earth could only have appeared by being created by a *supernatural* power.
4. There are no huge "missing links" in the fossil record of human evolution; it's pretty clear now that humans evolved from earlier species.
5. No one has ever seen evolution happening in a species; the theory is built on an assumed process never witnessed.
6. There are several plausible ways that life could have evolved, by strictly *natural* means, from nonliving material.
7. A lot of famous scientists reject the theory of evolution today.
8. Solid evidence from astronomy and geology show the earth is over 4 billion years old—not just 10,000 years or so.
9. The universe had to be designed by a supernatural intelligence. It is too perfectly arranged to be due to blind luck.
10. Even very complicated forms of life could have evolved by chance, given the enormous amount of time available.
11. "Creation science" is not a science at all, but a religious doctrine that has no place in a science curriculum.
12. I believe the creationists' explanation of how life appeared on earth, and not the theory of evolution.

Note: Items are answered on a -4 to +4 basis. Scores are computed to indicate antievolution beliefs. Items 2, 4, 6, 8, 10, and 11 are, therefore, con-traits for which the scoring key is reversed.

---

assessment of "Evolution versus Creation Science." You can see that half the items on the scale, reproduced in exhibit 7.2, support evolution. The others present arguments (sometimes factually inaccurate) commonly raised against evolution, or else they simply endorse creation science.

Summed scores over the twelve responses could roam from 12 (pro-evolution) to 108 (pro–creation science), and averaged 60 for the sample as a whole—precisely on the neutral point.[2] The fifty-one atheists had an unexpectedly high median of 38. They (modestly) supported the theory of evolution on most items, but lamentably agreed (median of 6) with the old antievolutionary canard that Darwin claimed humans had descended from monkeys.[3] They also came up neutral on whether creation science should be considered a science or a religious doctrine. The fundamentalists on the other hand had pro–creation science medians of 9 on nearly all the items, and their average scaled the scale at 95. They only blinked on the earth's age, with many of them agreeing that our planet has been around for over 4 billion years, not just ten thousand.

Attitudes toward Homosexuals

The next topic tests our acumen but little more. Will atheists feel the same way about gays and lesbians as fundamentalists do? Not likely, huh? We measured attitudes toward homosexuals with the twelve items shown in exhibit 7.3, which assess condemning, vindictive, and punitive sentiments toward this group. Again, half the items are worded so that the anti-homosexual response is to disagree. High scores indicate hostility toward gays and lesbians.

With scores potentially running between 12 and 108 and the neutral point being 60 again, the median for the whole sample of parents landed at 38—solidly in the tolerant range.[4] All of the items had pro–gay and lesbian averages, including no. 3 about the contentious issue of homosexual marriage.

The atheist parents put up an even more accepting average of 23. Their highest item score (a median of 3 on the 1–9 basis) came on the issue of gay marriage. Will it amaze you to learn that the highly fundamentalist parents rang up an overall average of 70, on the rejecting side of the neutral point? They proved most rejecting (medians of 9) in opposing marriage among homosexuals and in calling homosexuality an abomination in the sight of God.

But why should atheist parents be so accepting of homosexuals? Few of them, if any, would be gay or lesbian themselves. Being an atheist may spare you the homophobia that some religions reinforce, but it does not, in any obvious way, make you pro-homosexual.[5] We may have an explanation later on.

Racial and Ethnic Prejudice

What about racial and ethnic prejudice? We have used a twenty-item scale, shown in exhibit 7.4, to measure such attitudes for many years. You can see that it "names

Exhibit 7.3
The Attitudes toward Homosexuals Scale

1. I won't associate with known homosexuals if I can help it.
2. Homosexuals have been treated unfairly for centuries, and should be treated today the same as everyone else.
3. If two homosexuals want to get married, the law should let them.
4. Homosexuals should be locked up to protect society.
5. Homosexuals should never be given positions of trust in caring for children.
6. I would join an organization even though I knew it had homosexuals in its membership.
7. In many ways, the AIDS disease currently killing homosexuals is just what they deserve.
8. I wouldn't mind being seen smiling and chatting with a known homosexual.
9. Homosexuals have a perfect right to their lifestyle, if that's the way they want to live.
10. Homosexuals should be forced to take whatever treatments science can come up with to make them normal.
11. People should feel sympathetic and understanding of homosexuals, who are unfairly attacked in our society.
12. Homosexuality is "an abomination in the sight of God."

Note: Items are answered on a -4 to +4 basis. Scores are computed to reflect hostility toward homosexuals. Keying is reversed for Items 2, 3, 6, 8, 9, and 11.

names" and invokes some of the common negative stereotypes of our culture. Doubtless people realize, when they are answering it, that we are trying to find out how prejudiced they are. Amazingly, they tell us—at least to some extent, especially when they are answering anonymously.

Scores on the Manitoba Ethnocentrism scale can total anywhere from 20 to 180. The entire sample of 836 parents had a median of 74, decidedly on the nonprejudiced side of the midpoint (100). The fifty-one atheists among them had a median score exactly ten points lower (64), while the median of the fifty-one highly fundamentalist parents landed ten points above the group average (84). Only seven of the atheists and fourteen of the fundamentalists had scores as high as 100 or more.

While statistically significant, the 64 versus 84 difference seems inconsequential compared with the chasms we have usually found separating scores from these extremely different groups. But it affirms the larger relationship between religious fundamentalism and racial/ethnic prejudice that we mentioned at the beginning of chapter 6. Although small, the correlations have popped up in study after study.

Exhibit 7.4
The Manitoba Ethnocentrism Scale

1. There are entirely too many people from the wrong sorts of places being admitted into Canada now.
2. We should take in more refugees fleeing political persecution by repressive governments.
3. If we don't watch out, Asians will control our economy and we'll be the "coolies."
4. If Sikhs who join the RCMP want to wear turbans instead of the usual hat, that's fine.
5. It is good to live in a country where there are so many minorities present, such as blacks, Asians, and aboriginals.
6. "Foreign" religions like Buddhism, Hinduism, and Islam are just as good as Christianity, all things considered.
7. As a group, aboriginal people are naturally lazy, dishonest, and lawless.
8. The more we let people from all over the world into our country, the better.
9. Black people are, by their nature, more violent and "primitive" than others.
10. Jews can be trusted as much as everyone else.
11. People from India who have come to Canada have mainly brought disease, ignorance, and crime with them.
12. Every person we let in from overseas means either another Canadian won't be able to find a job, or another foreigner will go on welfare here.
13. Canada should guarantee that French language rights exist across the country.
14. It is a waste of time to train certain races for good jobs; they simply don't have the drive and determination it takes to learn a complicated skill.
15. Canada has much to fear from the Japanese, who are as cruel as they are ambitious.
16. There is nothing wrong with intermarriage among the races.
17. Arabs are too emotional, and they don't fit in well in our country.
18. Aboriginal people should keep on protesting and demonstrating until they get just treatment in Canada.
19. Many minorities are spoiled; if they really wanted to improve their lives, they'd get off welfare and get jobs.
20. It's a sad fact that many minorities have been persecuted in our country, and some are still treated very unfairly.

Note: Items are answered on a -4 to +4 basis. Scores are computed to indicate prejudice. Keying for items 2, 4, 5, 6, 8, 10, 13, 16, 18, and 20 is reversed.

Why should this be? We can understand the hostility toward gays and lesbians among some religious persons, since their religion not only gets out the vote against homosexual marriage, but flat out condemns homosexuality itself. But what religion today advocates closing the door to Asian immigrants, or spews stereotypes from the pulpit about aboriginal peoples, blacks, Jews, and Japanese? Part of the answer, as mentioned earlier, lay in fundamentalists' relative lack of education. It may also be due to the early ethnocentric training that children get when raised in "true believer" homes. But this depressing unchristian prejudice among upstanding Christians simmers for a third reason as well. And this third factor solves the mystery that has developed over the past few pages: Why do atheists appear less prejudiced against minorities in our society than most people are?

Right-Wing Authoritarianism

Right-wing authoritarianism is defined as the covariation of three kinds of attitudes: authoritarian submission (to established authorities), authoritarian aggression (against anyone the authorities target), and conventionalism (adhering to the social conventions thought to be endorsed by society and the established authorities). The trait is called "right-wing" because the submission occurs to established authorities. (You could have a left-wing authoritarianism among people who submit to revolutionary authorities.) For a full discussion of this definition, see Bob Altemeyer, *Right-Wing Authoritarianism* (Winnipeg: University of Manitoba Press, 1968), pp. 147–55.

Right-wing authoritarianism is measured by the RWA scale. The latest version is presented in exhibit 7.5. If you look at item 1, you might agree that it combines the three elements of the definition: "Our country desperately needs a mighty leader" (*authoritarian submission*) "who will do what has to be done to destroy" (*authoritarian aggression*) "the radical new ways and sinfulness that are ruining us" (*conventionalism*). All of the items on the RWA scale tap at least two of these elements, and many were composed to capture all three sentiments. A great deal of evidence over many years from many places around the world indicates that the RWA scale measures the "authoritarian follower" personality. Such individuals would make good rank-and-file members of a right-wing totalitarian movement and lift, if they could, a dictator to power.[6] (We also now have a scale that assesses people's inclination to be an authoritarian leader.)[7]

The 836 parents in the sample had a median score of 84 on the RWA scale, well on the unauthoritarian side of the neutral point of 100.[8] The fifty-one atheists among them averaged a very low 51, which the fundamentalists more than doubled at 135.[9] But wait. Many of the statements in exhibit 7.5 refer to religion, religious morality, and even atheists. Have we, with trumpets blaring and banners flying, magnificently Discovered The Fantastically Obvious, that religious people have more religious attitudes than atheists do?

It may involve more than just that. You see, another explanation of the findings says that religious content found its way onto the RWA scale in the first place because,

Exhibit 7.5
The 20-Item Right-Wing Authoritarianism Scale

1. Our country desperately needs a mighty leader who will do what has to be done to destroy the radical new ways and sinfulness that are ruining us.
2. Gays and lesbians are just as healthy and moral as anybody else.
3. It is always better to trust the judgment of the proper authorities in government and religion than to listen to the noisy rabble-rousers in our society who are trying to create doubt in people's minds.
4. Atheists and others who have rebelled against the established religions are no doubt every bit as good and virtuous as those who attend church regularly.
5. The only way our country can get through the crisis ahead is to get back to our traditional values, put some tough leaders in power, and silence the troublemakers spreading bad ideas.
6. There is absolutely nothing wrong with nudist camps.
7. Our country *needs* free thinkers who have the courage to defy traditional ways, even if this upsets many people.
8. Our country will be destroyed someday if we do not smash the perversions eating away at our moral fiber and traditional beliefs.
9. Everyone should have their own lifestyle, religious beliefs, and sexual preferences, even if it makes them different from everyone else.
10. The "old-fashioned ways" and the "old-fashioned values" still show the best way to live.
11. You have to admire those who challenged the law and the majority's view by protesting for women's abortion rights, for animal rights, or to abolish school prayer.
12. What our country really needs is a strong, determined leader who will crush evil, and take us back to our true path.
13. Some of the best people in our country are those who are challenging our government, criticizing religion, and ignoring the "normal way things are supposed to be done."
14. God's laws about abortion, pornography, and marriage must be strictly followed before it is too late, and those who break them must be strongly punished.
15. There are many radical, immoral people in our country today, who are trying to ruin it for their own godless purposes, whom the authorities should put out of action.
16. A "woman's place" should be wherever she wants to be. The days when women are submissive to their husbands and social conventions belong strictly in the past.
17. Our country will be great if we honor the ways of our forefathers, do what the authorities tell us to do, and get rid of the "rotten apples" who are ruining everything.
18. There is no "ONE right way" to live life; everybody has to create their *own* way.
19. Homosexuals and feminists should be praised for being brave enough to defy "traditional" family values.
20. This country would work a lot better if certain groups of troublemakers would just shut up and accept their group's traditional place in society.

Note: Items are answered on a -4 to +4 basis. Scores are computed to indicate levels of right-wing authoritarianism. Keying for items 2, 4, 6, 7, 9, 11, 13, 15, 16, and 19 is reversed.

in our culture, much authoritarian submission, authoritarian aggression, and conventionalism arises from religious instruction. That is, the huge difference in RWA scores between atheists and fundamentalists does not reflect divergent religious outlooks so much as it reflects disparity in underlying right-wing authoritarianism.

How can one "pit" these two interpretations of the gap in RWA scores to see which one rules? Rather simply. If the items on the scale that mention religion and religious morality are mainly measuring religious sentiment, as distinguished from the attitudes of an authoritarian follower, then answers to those items will highly correlate with (go together with) answers to a scale that definitely measures religious attitudes—such as the Religious Fundamentalism scale. But if those statements are mainly tapping authoritarian submission, authoritarian aggression, and conventionalism, responses to them will correlate highly and *better* with the other items on the RWA scale, including those that do not mention religion. And that is what you find when you do a "PIT scan" of the inner workings of the scale.

To put it another way, in our culture religion can lend itself to serving authoritarian ends, as it has in other cultures. It does not always, of course, nor probably in most people. But right-wing authoritarians in our culture tend to be highly "religious" because religion has been the authority-supported, conventional source of moral judgments, social norms, do's and don'ts. In particular, fundamentalism appears to be the authoritarian response to the religious impulse insofar as it stresses authoritarian submission, authoritarian aggression, and conventionalism.

We can test this proposition further by looking at cultures that imbue atheism. Who scored highly on the RWA scale in the Soviet Union? Supporters of the Communist Party did, for the obvious reason that party doctrine was espoused by the established authorities in their society.[10] Those championing democratic reforms scored quite low. Hence the connection is not lashed between authoritarianism and religion, but between authoritarianism and whatever the established authorities in your culture assert.

Let's test this interpretation in yet another way. If things shake down the way we have suggested, then many of the relationships we found between religious fundamentalism and other things, such as hostility toward homosexuals and racial/ethnic prejudice, are really relationships between right-wing authoritarianism and those prejudices. Fundamentalism is simply riding piggy-back on the more powerful, underlying personality trait of being an authoritarian follower. What would happen if we could somehow separate the two, and control for (i.e., statistically eliminate) the influence of authoritarianism when we are examining those puzzling connections between fundamentalism and prejudice?

It may seem magical but a very simple statistical technique, called a partial correlation analysis, lets us pull apart the intertwined, complicated parts of people's beliefs and personalities to see what is the dog and what is the tail. When we use this procedure, we find that if fundamentalists were not so authoritarian as a group, they would not be prejudiced at all. In fact, the relatively small number of un-authoritarian fundamentalists usually seem quite open-minded and tolerant. But for most fundamentalists, their prejudices usually reflect their underlying right-wing authoritarianism. True, religion probably helped shape their authoritarianism, but so did other experiences in their lives. If we want to understand their prejudices (and their political leanings, and much, much else), the real story lay in their authoritarianism.

Which brings us back to our central topic—atheists. Remember our little mystery? We wondered why atheists would score *lower* than most people in hostility toward homosexuals and in racial/ethnic prejudice. Now we have our answer: atheists are, of course, relatively unauthoritarian. Do they submit readily to established authorities? Are they hostile toward the groups that the authorities do not like? Do they cling to social conventional? No, Nope, Uh-uh. So if much prejudice springs from authoritarianism—and evidence indicates that most of the highly prejudiced people we find in our culture are either authoritarian leaders or authoritarian followers[11]—then it makes sense that relatively unauthoritarian people would be relatively unprejudiced.

And a great deal more. But that takes us to the next chapter.

NOTES

1. See Bob Altemeyer and Bruce Hunsberger, *Amazing Conversions: Why Some Turn to Faith and Others Abandon Religion* (Amherst, NY: Prometheus Books, 1997), pp. 243–47.

2. Over the entire sample of 836 parents, the mean inter-item correlation among the twelve statements was 0.344, producing an alpha reliability coefficient equal to 0.865.

3. Charles Darwin proposed that human beings arose from an ancient member of the anthropomorphous apes (gorillas, chimpanzees, orangutans, and gibbons), which had diverged from the evolutionary line that produced monkeys millions of years earlier. See chapter 6 of *The Descent of Man*. The discovery of the australopithecines has given a face, so to speak, to these progenitors, who were neither monkeys nor chimpanzees.

4. The mean inter-item correlation on the scale was 0.479, yielding an alpha of 0.915. Scores on the Attitudes toward Homosexuals scale have dropped (i.e., become more pro-homosexual) dramatically over the past dozen years in Manitoba samples. The major reasons cited by students and parents were (1) they have gotten to know gay or lesbian persons and realized they are just like everyone else except for sexual orientation; (2) they have learned of scientific evidence on the biological origins of sexual orientation; and (3) they have been turned off by anti-homosexual hostility. See Bob Altemeyer, "Changes in Attitudes toward Homosexuals," *Journal of Homosexuality* 42 (2001): 63–75.

5. Some religions teach their members "to hate sin, but love the sinner." This seems a lot to ask of followers inclined to blame sin on, and punish, the sinner. Does acceptance of this teaching actually make any difference? In 1991 we compared the Attitudes toward Homosexuals of high fundamentalist students who earlier expressed agreement with "We should hate sin, but love the sinner" with other high fundamentalists who disagreed with the statement. If people take the "love the sinner" message to heart, the former should be less hostile. But there was almost a statistically significant difference in the "wrong" direction, with the endorsers being *more* hostile toward homosexuals than those who disagreed with the admonition. Thus the endorsement probably falls in the category of lip service.

6. See chapter 1 of B. Altemeyer, *The Authoritarian Specter* (Cambridge, MA: Harvard University Press, 1996), for a summary of this evidence up to that point.

7. The "authoritarian leader" kind of personality seems to be well measured by the Social Dominance Orientation scale developed by Felicia Pratto of the University of Connecticut and Jim Sidanius at UCLA. (F. Pratto, J. Sidanius, L. M. Stallworth, and B. F. Malle, "Social Dominance Orientation: A Personality Variable Predicting Social and Political Attitudes," *Journal of Personality and Social Psychology* 67 [1994]: 741–63.) See B. Altemeyer, "The 'Other Authoritarian Personality,'" in *Advances in Experimental Social Psychology*, ed. M. Zanna (New York: Academic Press, 1998). If that interests you, see B. Altemeyer, "Highly Dominating, Highly Authoritarian Personalities," *Journal of Social Psychology* 144 (2004): 421–47 for further investigations of the people seemingly likely to become leaders of right-wing movements.

8. The mean intercorrelation among the twenty RWA scale items for the entire sample equaled 0.321, which produced an alpha coefficient of 0.904.

9. Here are the means, standard deviations, and tests of significance for the Manitoba parent comparisons in this chapter. Creation Science scores: Atheists = 38.4 (13.4), Fundamentalists = 91.2 (12.5), $t = 20.6$, $p < 0.001$; Attitudes toward Homosexuals scores: Atheists = 28.1 (17.4), Fundamentalists = 68.3 (13.8), $t = 12.9$, $p < 0.001$; Manitoba Ethnocentrism scores: Atheists = 61.5 (29.7), Fundamentalists = 81.2 (23.6), $t = 3.71$, $p < 0.001$; Right-Wing Authoritarianism scores: Atheists = 53.1 (21.4), Fundamentalists = 133.8 (20.1), $t = 19.6$, $p < 0.001$.

10. See S. McFarland, V. Ageyev, and M. Abalakina-Paap, "Authoritarianism in the Former Soviet Union," *Journal of Personality and Social Psychology* 63 (1992): 1004–10. Also see Altemeyer, *The Authoritarian Specter*, pp. 122–30.

11. See Altemeyer, "The 'Other Authoritarian Personality.'"

CHAPTER 8

SUMMARY AND PREDICTIONS ABOUT "ORDINARY" AMERICAN ATHEISTS

It's time to see where we have gotten to, and add up what we have discovered about active American atheists. Then we shall try to line up the implications of our findings for the broader domain of American atheism. But first, let's have a little fun and tear this study to pieces, limb by limb.

We can start with the samples used. One of them commands the spotlight, that drawn from the six San Francisco area atheists clubs. The other groups mainly put the 253 Bay Area reports in perspective. Are all of those 253 *active* atheists? True, they belong to organizations that are bringing lawsuits, holding meetings, staging demonstrations, and publicizing their cause. But some of the people who kindly filled out our surveys have never done anything along these lines and probably have not got a militant bone in their bodies. A few said their names appear on the mailing lists because they like to keep up with what active atheists are doing. Some of them told us they go to meetings mainly to socialize with people holding similar views—the same reason some people go to church—or else to argue. A couple of our Alabama and Idaho respondents do not even belong to an atheists club. They just were known to be atheists by the local club president, who kindly pushed our survey in their direction. So while these samples, as a group, undoubtedly advocate more than most American atheists do, some of the respondents do nothing more than keep their names on an atheist mailing list.

We must also acknowledge all the people who declined to participate. Unquestionably, the results would be different if they had chimed in. Did older atheists tend to volunteer more? Those raised in nonreligious homes? Those who had suffered most? If a big self-selection bias shapes a sample, you can get almost any result imaginable. Maybe the authors of this book are not as dumb as we say they are, just the victims of bad sampling luck. Maybe some sneaky factor that provoked the most dogmatic, least zealous, and most ethnocentric atheists to return our surveys sabotaged us. Who can say it didn't?

We must also keep in mind the many ways American and Canadian atheists probably differ. *Stigma*: If you live in a city of any size in Canada and do not go to church because you are an atheist, most of your theist neighbors will not notice because they do not go either. Nor will they likely care why you sleep in. *Militancy*: So far as we know, no active atheists clubs exist anywhere in Canada. Canadian atheists have little to be militant about. *Age*: Being a Canadian parent in your late forties in 2002 means you were eight to sixteen years old during the cauldron years of the civil rights movement and Vietnam War protests, whereas our Bay Area correspondents were ten years older, going through college at those times, and often in the front lines. *Education*: The Manitoba samples went to school less, even though higher education was more available to them. *National Differences*: Americans live in a more turbulent, violent society than Canadians do. Canada has a parliamentary system of government, a more mixed economy, and plays its national games on ice. One country drinks more beer (we don't know which). And so on, ad infinitum. Given all the discrepancies, don't we have to be quite cautious when interpreting differences between San Francisco atheists and Manitoba atheists in "thermometer" readings and reactions to "ancient scrolls"?

Another set of doubts arises from the way we collected the data, through surveys. How do we know who really filled out the questionnaires? How do we know they told the truth? How do we know they know the truth? How do we know they even knew what we were asking?

Surveys have inherent problems, don't they? (A) Words mean different things to different people. Questionnaires have an advantage over interviews because the researcher does not interact with the respondent and so cannot influence the answers. But they can also produce a false picture precisely because the researcher does not interact with the respondent and so cannot explain what the questions mean. (B) Even when meaning is unmistakable, tired or unmotivated participants can give you gibberish, and angry subjects can give you nightmares. (C) Subjects will give you different answers on Monday and Tuesday if their mood changes sufficiently in the meantime. (D) As well, people try to make themselves look good any day of the week, and (E) if they know you are studying them as members of some group they will often try to make the group look good. (F) Respondents can give you the opposite of their opinions because they miss a word like "not" in an item. (G) Less educated subjects tend to give emphatic answers, lots of +4s and -4s, even when they have no opinion. (H) Informants tend to think survey items reflect the researchers' opinions, and the "right answer" is yes. (I) Some subjects, the yea-sayers, answer mostly with +1, +2, +3, and +4 in any event. (J) Others, like two-year-olds, say no to almost everything.

Such serious problems cannot be blown off, but we can catch a little reassurance from the details of this study. Assuming all six hundred of the San Francisco packets actually reached the person addressed, we received completed surveys from almost half (even though some proved to be agnostics, not atheists). The Alabama/Idaho atheists responded at a 70 percent clip. These represent very good return rates for a mail-back survey.[1] How likely would you be to complete a long questionnaire that pokes all around in your personal philosophy, and even challenges it, sent to you by someone you never heard of, with not a thing in it for you—not even "You may have won a $10,000 watch!"? Undoubtedly the cooperation of the atheists clubs made all the difference. But we nevertheless hopped, skipped, and jumped when the returns kept pouring in.

These return rates mean that, while the results would be changed somewhat if more people had responded, they probably would not change much. To take the most vulnerable case, the San Francisco atheists *might* have looked appreciably less dogmatic if the other half of the surveys had been returned. But that is a mighty big "might." We might be dumb, but it would be dumb and dumber to make the excuse that we didn't get the results we expected because we didn't hear from the right people.

As for the differences between the American and Canadian samples, the point is well taken, and the two can only be compared with great caution. But the two extremes of the parent sample *can* be directly compared, and doing so gives us the footing for predicting what ordinary American atheists would be like, compared with high fundamentalists, in the United States. We shall be doing so soon.

Finally, what about all the problems inherent in doing survey research? Respondents bring some things with them that researchers cannot do anything about, such as their reading comprehension and their mood when answering. But most of the other problems listed above can be addressed and even controlled. Motivational problems seem to be helped by promises of feedback and statements like, "We would only want you to participate if you freely choose to do so." The American atheists may have been additionally beckoned by the statement that while religious people had been investigated extensively, nonbelievers such as themselves had never been studied before. Making the surveys anonymous probably cooled down the desire to make a good personal impression. We tried to address the "make the group look good" effect and tendency to guess what the researchers want with the fifth paragraph of the explanatory letter, in which we pointed out the dangers and said, "We want *your* answers, whether you think they are representative of your club or not." You can emphasize **no**'s and NOT's in items, as we did. Yea-saying and nay-saying can be controlled by balancing personality tests and attitude surveys with equal numbers of pro-trait and con-trait items. That doesn't stop people from agreeing with everything they are asked, but all that agreeing cancels itself out when you add up the scores and does not affect the final tally.

Here's the bottom line on the scales: Most of the Top Ten problems listed above produce measurement error that weakens the stability, the *reliability* of test scores. Ambiguous wording, for example, will cause an item to mean different things to different people, different things to the same person on different occasions, and different things from other items on the scale trying to measure the same thing. A test's reliability can be assessed by various statistical rigmaroles, and can vary from 0.00 (which is abysmal, wretched; in fact it's so bad it's never happened) to 1.00 (absolutely perfect; in fact so perfect it also has never happened). If you look in statistic textbooks (go ahead, we'll wait), you will see that 0.80 is usually considered "adequate" or even "good" for a scale. (This field is not known for its high need for achievement; a reliability of 0.80 only has a "signal-to-noise ratio" of 4:1—that being the ratio of good information to misleading information from a test, or 0.80 divided by 0.20.) The best IQ tests boast a reliability of about 0.90 (which means the signal-to-noise ratio is a much more reassuring 9:1).

We have reported the reliability of responses to our various scales in the endnotes. Here they are again, given for all the samples that encountered the measure: Religious Fundamentalism: 0.92; Religious Doubts: 0.92, 0.91, and 0.92; Religious Emphasis: 0.98 and 0.98; DOGmatism: 0.85, 0.84, and 0.91; Religious Ethnocentrism: 0.87; Creation Science: 0.86; Attitudes toward Homosexuals: 0.92; and Right-Wing Authoritarianism: 0.90. You may have writhed in agony when you were answering the scales in this book, wondering, "What do they mean?!" But believe it or not, most people apparently do not writhe—not even atheists. If they did, we would get a lot more unanswered scales, and the answered ones would not have such high reliability. The years spent developing these measures have paid off.

SUMMARY OF FINDINGS ON "ACTIVE" AMERICAN ATHEISTS

We thus have a lot of apparently good survey data from atheists who belong to clubs in either the San Francisco area (N = 253) or else in Alabama or Idaho (N = 28). What can we say about them? Demographically, active atheism appears to be mostly an educated, "left-winger," old, guy, thing. Are they really atheists? Yes, down to their toenails. They not only reject the traditional Judeo-Christian God, but also any *super*natural being or power whatsoever. Furthermore, the Hidden Observer answers indicate that almost all of them have no doubts whatsoever about the nonexistence of a God, not even the secret, hidden, four-o'-clock-in-the-morning doubts that apparently rumble around in a lot of fundamentalists' minds. God does *not* exist, they very strongly believe. They *do* doubt the truth and worth of organized religion, racking up the highest scores on the twenty-item Religious Doubts scale we have ever seen. In the main they doubt religion for intellectual reasons, not because of emotional blows such as the death of a loved one. In the main, they simply found it all unbelievable.

How did they get this way? Most of them had very little religious upbringing as children. They may have had a nonbeliever mom or dad, but even if the parents believed in God, they had no interest in religion per se. Nevertheless, most of our informants acquired religion somewhere along the way, from friends, neighbors, or the culture in general. A small part of our sample in fact got religion from the get-go, as they grew up in intensely religious circumstances and experienced strong pressure to believe, believe, believe. The Alabama/Idaho participants encountered significantly more religious emphasis in childhood than those from San Francisco did, so the number of active atheists in the United States who might describe themselves as "recovering fundamentalists" might well be higher than our study showed.

However they got there, our future atheists began to wonder seriously about God and religion at some point in their lives because, usually, what they had been taught stopped making sense to them. This critical examination came earlier and was probably easier for the Bay Area atheists, typically beginning in the middle teen years. Those in Alabama and Idaho began to doubt around age eighteen, and it took them over twice as long on the average as the San Francisco participants (fourteen years versus six years) to decide, "Chuck it." Religion's big enemy in losing the battle for these minds proved not to be Satan, but its own scriptures, its various teachings, and its history. Most of our participants apparently worked things out by themselves, reading a lot but talking very little. Why did they abandon religion when so many people embrace it? For most, the roots ran pretty shallow to start with because of a weak family background. For those who had been firmly raised in a faith, the many times they heard theirs was the true religion may have created a love for the truth that surpasses all understanding—at least all understanding that the family religion could provide. We did not give out an IQ test in our study, but the atheists were probably quite bright as children who had been frequently rewarded for "getting the right answer."

We wish we had asked, "To what extent do you let other people know you are an atheist?" because some of our informants mentioned that no one knew what they really believed. Others seemed quite judicious about whom they let know what. Most of our active atheists felt they had paid some sort of price for their disbelief in God, and the more active they were, the more they had been avoided, excluded, or harassed. Many atheists indicated they felt stigmatized for being nonbelievers.

Turning to the question of what active atheists are like, we were surprised to find consistent evidence of dogmatism in their thinking. They scored much higher on the twenty-item DOG scale than we expected. Nearly all of them said that scientifically validated evidence confirming the Gospel accounts of Jesus' public life, death, and resurrection would have no effect at all on their beliefs about his divinity. And most said nothing conceivable could lead them to believe in the traditional God. We tried to understand these results, observing that certain items on the DOG scale would unfairly make elderly atheists look dogmatic, that a "Roman file" obviously would not *prove* Jesus' divinity, that clearly these atheists were not dogmatic when they gave up their religious beliefs, and they may feel entitled to their certainty because they base their beliefs on science. Or perhaps the suffering they had endured had nailed their thinking into place. But ultimately we were confounded by the consistent evidence for dogmatism.

We also tried to measure zealotry in a number of ways to see if atheists would show the sort of proselytizing fervor for which some fundamentalists are known. We asked our informants how they would advise a teen who had received a religious upbringing but was now beginning to question things. Most of our San Francisco and Alabama/Idaho participants would have said something that, in our judgment, would have promoted atheism. Roughly half of them revealed they would want the teen to become an atheist. But most of them indicated they would not try to lead the teen in this direction. Instead, they would want the individual to make up her own mind. This indeed was the tack most of the atheists said they took with their own children. And when asked how they would react to a hypothetical law that would teach atheism in public schools, a solid majority said it would be a bad law, that no particular religious viewpoint should be taught in such a place. Overall, then, we found that while these active atheists may be very involved in protecting their own rights, they gave little indication of wanting to convert others to their beliefs. No one probably takes up a collection at atheist meetings to support missionaries.

Our booklets contained two attempts at measuring religious ethnocentrism. The first presented six items about associating with religious people, voting for religious politicians, and having their children attend some religion's youth group with friends. Overall we found the atheists rather standoffish in these regards, reacting most against the notion of devout persons teaching their children in elementary school. Second, we asked our samples to rate various religious groups on a 0 to 100 scale. The atheists really liked themselves and really disliked fundamentalists—to practically the maximum amount the scale would allow. So these active atheists appear highly prejudiced about people based upon religious affiliation.

And that, in a three-page nutshell, is what we found in our survey of active American atheists. It seems rather paltry when condensed to this degree, does it not? Partly that's because of the condensation, but it also reflects our conscious decision to try to measure each trait several ways. We knew that, as the first such study of these very interesting people, everything would be "news," and we wanted to get it right.

You may have noticed that the summary above speaks strictly in terms of the absolute level of the atheists' scores, not how they looked compared with anyone else. We have data on Manitoba parents, but none on the "anyone else" of greatest interest, active American religious fundamentalists. How would they score on dogmatism, zealotry, and religious ethnocentrism? Lower? As high? Higher? Those questions can, in principle, be answered by other researchers in the near future. We wish them well. But if you are inclined to bet that the active fundamentalists will look *better* than the active atheists did, the results of the Manitoba parent study indicate you are entitled to good odds in your favor.

Even if active American fundamentalists look as dogmatic, zealous, and ethnocentric as their enemies believe they are, some of the data in hand cannot bring much joy to the groups that provided them. The numbers imply that, in some respects at least, the people who so intensely oppose and dislike each other from each end of the religious-belief spectrum have some things in common. There seem to be fundamentalists at each pole, and while it would not bother some Baptists, Jehovah's Witnesses, Pentecostals, and so on to be called that, it must be distressing to many atheists. Yet it seems that other atheists know such are among them. Recall that we added "Fundamentalist Atheists" to the list of Thermometer targets to be evaluated by the Alabama/Idaho sample, while also providing an opt-out response, "This last one does not exist." Only eight of the twenty-eight respondents opted out. The other twenty had an opinion of these people and gave them a median rating of 40 on the

0–100 scale. So some atheists apparently believe that they have "fundamentalist" nonbelievers in their ranks, and do not particularly value them.

All we are saying is what the Prime Mover of this study, Chris Lindstrom, wrote when we said our study would have to be strictly a scientific study done without any biasing influence from the sponsoring clubs: "I fully understand . . . that any study would most likely reveal some unflattering portraits as well as flattering ones . . . [But] it's better to be (and be seen as) human beings." Our respondents are, in the data, superhumans in some respects we think. In other respects, well, Chris proved a better prophet than we. But who isn't?

WHAT ARE ORDINARY AMERICAN ATHEISTS LIKE?

Since we have nothing to lose (one of us is now deceased and the other is so near the end he has forgotten proper grammar) we shall close this chapter with our top ten predictions about ordinary American atheists. By ordinary atheists we mean that vast "bulk" of the tiny part of the American population that believes God does not exist. We mean people such as our fifty-one Manitoba parent atheists, people who do not belong to an atheist organization and thus could not show up in our USA samples. We mean, probably, a lot of the people reading this sentence. (Brace yourself; you're about to be repeatedly clapped on the back.) For obvious reasons we cannot do these studies, but researchers with access to American samples can. All they need is a large enough group so that the culled 3 percent (more or less, depending on the locale) yields enough atheists to give our hunches a fair run for their money. (Hint: Make this part of a larger study, even though it means you will have to accept a large grant, so you can do something useful with the other 97 percent of the surveys.)

Our predictions are based on the belief, expounded in chapter 7, that *right-wing authoritarianism* explains many of the things that people think and do. (We assume this reflexively, it must be admitted, because the one of us still alive and kicking and writing invested a career in that belief.) Table 8.1 lists twenty rather well-established (and often strong) relationships between scores on the Right-Wing Authoritarianism (RWA) scale and various behaviors.[2] We believe ordinary American atheists will score appreciably lower than most people on the RWA scale, because nonbelievers always have scored lower as a group in our samples. In fact, atheists may be one of the least authoritarian groups you can find. Because they score so low, much else follows—it would seem.

We say, "It would seem" because crack logicians will point out a tragic flaw in our thinking. While we learned in geometry that two things equal to the same thing must themselves be equal, it does *not* always follow that two things correlated with the same thing will be correlated with each other. Especially when the correlations are weak. So, it may be true that atheists *tend* to be relatively unauthoritarian, and it is well established that unauthoritarian people *tend* to be nondogmatic, but atheists are not automatically nondogmatic—as, indeed, we have seen. All those statements

---

Table 8.1
Summary of Scientific Findings Regarding Low RWAs

Compared to others, persons who score on the low end of the RWA scale are significantly *more* likely to:

1. Condemn unfair and illegal abuses of power by government authorities.
2. Distrust leaders who are untrustworthy.
3. Defend constitutional guarantees of liberty, such as the Bill of Rights.
4. Punish the crime when sentencing criminals; administer justice fairly, regardless of who the criminal is.
5. Hold authorities who commit crimes and people who attack minorities responsible for their acts.
6. Not rely on physical punishment as a way to correct behavior.
7. Resist government pressure to help persecute target groups.
8. Be understanding of those who have made mistakes and suffered.
9. Have well-integrated, noncompartmentalized minds.
10. Avoid using double standards in their judgments.
11. Not be hypocrites.
12. Be unprejudiced toward racial, ethnic, nationalistic, and linguistic minorities.
13. Accept homosexuals as people like anyone else and condemn "gay-bashing."
14. Support feminism.
15. Be less conforming to the opinions of others, and not be a yea-sayer, nor believe strongly in group cohesiveness and "group loyalty."
16. Be aware of themselves. Realize their personal failings and be open to feedback about such failings.
17. Not trust someone merely because he tells them what they want to hear.
18. Not feel the world is a dangerous place nor be self-righteous.
19. Be nondogmatic and nonzealous.
20. Support "liberal" or "left-wing" political parties and movements.

---

are generalizations, and generalizations have exceptions and sometimes the exceptions all gang up in the place you least expect them and you're wrong.

A. Nevertheless, we predict that ordinary American atheists will object to abuses of power by government more than most people do. The abuses do not have to be directed at them, and need not involve religious issues. High RWAs on the other hand are much more accepting of such abuse, and usually trust untrustworthy authorities far too much and far too long, which they did during Watergate.

B. Given a chance to be punitive, we expect atheists to be less harsh than most people. RWA scale scores have correlated positively with delivering high electric shocks (supposedly) as punishment during a learning experiment, with being mean-spirited, with handing out stiff sentences in mock trials, and with being willing to help the government persecute not only radicals, Communists, feminists, and homosexuals, but also "conservatives" and even right-wing authoritarians. If ordinary American atheists do prove to be pretty *un*authoritarian as a group, they are likely to also prove relatively nonpunitive.

C. These ordinary atheists will also show more integrity in their thinking than most people do. While it has been easy to find situations in which high RWAs, with their rigidly compartmentalized thinking, reveal double standards in their decisions and act hypocritically, low RWAs typically do not. The reaction of the Manitoba parents to the "Teach Atheism/Fundamentalism in School" proposals illustrates this (see figure 5.1).

D. We expect ordinary American atheists to be relatively unprejudiced, because we think they will be unauthoritarian. Accordingly, they should score low on measures of ethnic/racial prejudice, such as the Manitoba Ethnocentrism scale. Will they be religiously ethnocentric? They'll show a modest preference for "Atheists" over "Fundamentalists" on the Thermometer measure, but nothing like that shown by our active atheists. See figure 6.1.

E. If this is not too obvious, atheists should prove more resistant to conformity pressure than most people do. For example, if you show a group of people the *average* of the answers that *group* previously gave to some questions, and then ask them to respond to the items again, high RWAs will shift their opinions toward the group average about twice as much as low RWAs will. They simply place a lot more value on being "normal." They also believe much more in group solidarity and loyalty. We (Believe it or not!) expect atheists to place very little value on being like everybody else.

F. Ordinary American atheists should demonstrate greater self-awareness than most people do. Low RWAs usually have a pretty accurate idea of how their beliefs and attitudes compare with those of their peers. High RWAs, on the other hand, have a much poorer idea, mistakenly thinking they are normal when they are not. In general, high RWAs show a great deal of self-blindness, considering themselves much better at good things, and much less inclined to do evil things, than they really are. If given a chance to discover unpleasant things about themselves, low RWAs typically say, "Show me the evidence," and high RWAs simply run away.[3]

G. We predict that ordinary atheists will prove more adept at critical thinking. Specifically, they will be careful about trusting people who might well be treated with suspicion. Studies have shown that high RWAs will believe the sincerity of communicators who tell the highs what they want to hear—even when the highs know these communicators are likely making up their "lines" for other reasons, including vote getting and greed. Lows on the other hand do not so automatically trust someone who says what lows want to hear, when the communicator's motives are suspect. (So if you were an unscrupulous politician, which song would you sing—the one the hard-to-bamboozle lows like, or the one the easy-sell highs buy? Would this not lead such politicians to head for the causes and parties favored by highs?)

H.   The major causes of authoritarian aggression appear to be fear, which instigates an aggressive act, and self-righteousness, which overcomes the normal prohibitions against hurting others and releases the hostility. We expect atheists, therefore, to have relatively little tendency to see the world as a dangerous place, and not to be particularly self-righteous.

I.   We predict that *ordinary* American atheists will have somewhat lower DOGmatism scores than most people. We think the high San Francisco and Alabama/Idaho DOG scores will not appear as often among less active American atheists, who will instead look more like the low DOG Manitoba parent atheists in figure 4.1. As well, ordinary American atheists will have little evangelical drive.

J.   American atheists will tend to favor "left-wing" political parties, movements and causes. High RWAs generally support "right-wing" parties and activities. In fact, the politicians in such parties are differentiated fairly well by the RWA scale. Surveys of over twelve hundred American state lawmakers found Republicans almost always scored higher on the RWA scale than Democrats did in the same assembly—nearly forty points higher on the average across nearly all of the states.

So that is what we expect studies of ordinary American atheists will find. If you want to see the studies that led to these predictions, see Bob Altemeyer, *The Authoritarian Specter* (Cambridge, MA: Harvard University Press, 1996). If you think these predictions are such sure things that testing them is unnecessary, see pages 300 to 302 of this work for some other RWA findings that will lead to chancier prognostications about ordinary American atheists. But we have been unseated often enough by experimental results to know that "sure things" often finish out of the money. Whatever the results, we are confident that the second, third, and further studies of atheists will confirm that they are every bit as interesting and worth understanding as any religious group. For if organized religion is slowly dying, the needs it tried to meet and the questions it tried to answer remain undiminished. If the atheists "win," they may inherit those tasks as their prize.

NOTES

1. You have probably heard of, and perhaps been influenced by, surveys that were ridiculously under-returned. A notorious example among behavioral scientists is Shere Hite's book, *Women and Love*, which was based on a 4.5 percent return rate of a questionnaire sent to over one hundred thousand women.

2. This list is adapted from pages 300 to 302 of Bob Altemeyer, *The Authoritarian Specter* (Cambridge, MA: Harvard University Press, 1996).

3. See B. Altemeyer, "To Thine Own Self Be Untrue: Self-Awareness in Authoritarians," *North American Journal of Psychology* 1 (1999): 157–64.

CHAPTER 9

AGNOSTICS AND INACTIVE BELIEVERS IN THE MANITOBA PARENT SAMPLE

The legendary observant reader knows that we have, to this point, blissfully ignored most of the data collected in our large sample of Manitoba parents. We have only talked about the fifty-one atheists and the fifty-one highest fundamentalists who popped up in that sample of 836. Are there not other groups of interest? Well yes, and two come to mind first because each has taken a nontraditional stand on religion: (A) agnostics and (B) theists who claim affiliation with a religion, but do not go to church. Who fills these ranks? How did they respond to the various probes in our survey? How do they compare with the atheists and high fundamentalists? What do their answers indicate about the distribution of traits such as dogmatism and zealotry within a large sample of adults from one locale? If we draw meaningful subsamples such as atheists, agnostics, inactive believers, and high fundamentalists from the large Manitoba parent sample, will we find the trends predicted in the last chapter, or be refuted once again? And if we then look at *all* the meaningful subsamples, which we shall do at the end of this chapter, will utter chaos reign or will a Great Pattern emerge?

Agnosticism is sometimes defined as the belief that one cannot *ever* know whether God exists. As noted in chapter 1 we have taken a softer line, defining agnosticism as neutrality on the matter, but with no stand on what the future might bring. This position (which happens to be the orientation of both authors) seems cowardly to some of our active American atheists who wrote things like, "Agnostics are too chicken to be atheists," "They lack the courage of their lack of conviction," and "Agnostics are afraid to take The Big Step." Some theists too might have a corresponding reaction to agnostics' lack of faith.

One could say that the Inactive Believers also teeter at a precipice: They claim to believe in the traditional God, but they never go to church. Still they often say they are Catholics, or Anglicans, or whatever they were raised to be. Are they, really? Are they not just one step from joining that fastest-growing group we met in the introduction, the "Nones"? Let us see, as we compare these two "Yeah, but not . . ." groups, disbelievers *but* not atheists, and believers *but* not at all active.

SEX, AGE, AND EDUCATION

A sizeable 183 of the 836 Manitoba parents answered our "Do you believe in the traditional God?" question by checking the alternative that ran, "I am an agnostic. I do not believe in the existence of this 'traditional' God, *nor* do I disbelieve in it." As with our fifty-one Manitoba parent atheists, 61 percent of whom were males, agnostics tended (54 percent) to be guys. Again like those atheists, the agnostics had a median age of forty-eight years. But they had gone to school for fourteen years compared to the atheists' fifteen.

These 183 agnostics were accompanied by an even larger assembly (or rather, non-assembly) of 199 inactive believers in the parent sample. As is usually true of believers, they tended to be women, by a 57 percent majority. Like the agnostics, they also averaged forty-eight years in age, but had only twelve years of formal education to their credit. The fifty-one highly fundamentalist believers, you might recall, also had a median age of forty-eight, and thirteen years of schooling on the average.

BELIEF IN THE TRADITIONAL GOD

As one would expect, disbelief and belief in the traditional God was a little less cut-and-dried in these not-so-extreme groups than it was among the Manitoba atheists and high fundamentalists. *Dis*belief thundered a few decibels lower among the agnostic parents than it had among the atheists, with "only" 85 percent of the answers to our seven questions about the traditional God (see chapter 2) being in the negative—compared with a virtually unanimous 99 percent No vote among the atheists. True, the agnostics almost solidly disbelieved in an almighty God who created the universe, who is aware of us and hears our prayers, and who will judge us. But a modest difference of opinion emerged over whether a thinking, self-aware God exists, who is eternal, and who is all-loving and all-good—although in every case at least 76 percent said, "No, I don't believe that." So, while some of the agnostics embraced a few aspects of the traditional God, they *all* rejected most of the attributes presented and can rightly be called nonbelievers.

The inactive believers swung in the opposite direction, with 74 percent of their answers to these same questions being, "Yes, that is true." They solidly believed in a thinking, self-aware deity who is eternal, aware of us, all-loving and all-good. About a third of them, however, doubted that God is almighty, and nearly half (48 percent) did not think God had created the universe or that God will eventually judge us. This faith-with-footnotes withers before that of the fifty-one fundamentalist parents, who boomed out a 98 percent Yes vote overall. The God of the inactive believers was about as aware, eternal, mindful, and good as the God of the fundamentalists, but not nearly as often an almighty creator who will someday judge us.[1]

To summarize then, the agnostics did not *dis*believe in God as strenuously as the atheists did, nor did the inactive believers embrace the traditional God as fervently as did the high fundamentalists. Both findings make sense, do they not?

RELIGIOUS DOUBTS

The agnostics and inactive believers also answered the twenty-item Religious Doubts scale, on which nonreligious persons would be expected to post high scores. We saw in chapter 2 that atheistic parents had considerable doubts about the validity and worth of religion, with their summed scores centering on 73. The fundamentalist parents on the other hand had virtually no qualms, owning at most to a nearly bedrock median of 18. Where, then, did our "in-between" groups land? In between, again. The agnostics posted a median Doubts score of 60, while the inactive believers doubted their way to a notable 47—lower than the agnostics yet harboring far more misgivings than the high fundamentalists.[2]

Poking a little deeper into the data, we find that the agnostics came in one notch below the atheists on most of the issues shown in exhibit 2.1. For example, the problem of evil triggered a median doubt of 4 among the atheists (on the 0 to 6 response scale), and the median among the agnostics landed at 3. But larger differences turned up between atheists and agnostics on some issues: the existence of God (naturally), the importance of bad things religions had done in the past, the intolerance of some religious people, the divine origins of the Bible, the contradictory nature of some teachings, and the way faith made people blind. The atheists almost exploded with a Doubting Thomas median of 5 on these issues—where 6 represented the highest possible doubt. The agnostics doubted, too, but not so intensely and not so often.

We were more surprised yet by the large difference between the inactive believers and the fundamentalists. This gap was due, un-doubtedly, to the extreme answers of the fundamentalists—usually a 0 no matter what the issue. But the inactive believers' doubts were ratcheted about two notches higher on most of the twenty items. The biggest spreads (three notches) appeared (1) over the way religious people sometimes pressured others to believe what they believed, (2) because of hypocrisy seen among religious people, (3) because of the intolerance shown toward other religions and groups such as homosexuals, (4) over whether there is an afterlife, and (5) the way faith made people blind. Both the fundamentalists and the inactives believe in God, but the inactives have much greater doubts about organized religion and the people who appear religious—which, we shall see, helps explain their absence from church.

ROOTS OF AGNOSTICISM AND INACTIVITY

We saw in chapter 3 that active American atheists usually came from nonreligious backgrounds. Does the connection between childhood training and adult religiousness appear in our Manitoba parents?

Most of the parents, reared some forty to fifty years ago, reported they *had* been raised in a religion. Only 12 percent of the eventual Manitoba atheists and only 11 percent of the eventual agnostics said they had *no* home religion. The inactive believers (3 percent) and fundamentalists (0 percent) were even less likely to have been reared in no faith. Looking then at the home religions of these four groups, they generally follow the distribution in the overall sample with one exception: most of the high fundamentalists had been raised Mennonites (28 percent) or Fundamentalist Protestants (35 percent), although each group composed only 7 percent of the total sample. But no religion was especially likely, or unlikely, to produce atheists, agnostics, or inactives.

Because of space limitations in the booklet, the Manitoba parents only received ten of the twenty Religious Emphasis items shown in exhibit 3.1, and answered them on a 0 to 5 basis. The median for the *entire* sample of parents eked up to 18 (where the maximum would be $10 \times 5 = 50$), indicating religion had been emphasized less than "mildly" to them on the average while they were growing up. But those who eventually became atheists had heard only whispers about religion, having a median of 8. The eventual agnostics came in barely higher at 10, and the inactive believers, 17. Do you expect the fundamentalists to have experienced much greater emphasis on religion? You are right: 37.[3]

Which just goes to reinforce the "You reap what you sow" conclusion from chapter 3. The atheists and agnostics had but token backgrounds in religion, while the fundamentalists had been fairly immersed. This leaves the inactive believers, whose median approximated the (low) value of the sample as a whole. The inactives received enough religious instruction to develop a lasting belief in God—with the qualifications we have seen. But they have no time for organized religion. Again, we shall see why as we consider further findings from the Manitoba parent sample.

DOGMATISM

We saw in chapter 4 that the fifty-one Manitoba atheists had a median score of 65 on the twenty-item DOGmatism scale, and the highly fundamentalist parents averaged 126. The agnostics (median of 58) and the Inactive Believers (69) straddled the atheists.[4]

Each Manitoba parent also received a version of the "Ancient Scrolls" measure, the version depending on how religious their student-children said their parents were. Most of the *atheist* parents accordingly got the Roman File edition supporting the existence of Jesus, and we saw in chapter 4 that 64 percent of them said such evidence would not increase their belief in Jesus' divinity. These atheists' posttest responses to the question as to whether Jesus was the Son of God usually matched their pretest answer of -4. Most of the *fundamentalists* in turn got the Attis version, which cast strong doubt on the very existence of Jesus. But this had no effect whatsoever on the beliefs of the fundamentalists, with 93 percent of them saying they would believe in Jesus just as much as before—which was usually very strongly.

What about the agnostics? The most common pretest response of the 141 agnostics who received the Roman File version had *not* been the atheists' -4. Instead, most of them (N = 72) answered with an agnostic 0 (i.e., neutral). After reading the Roman File they were asked what they would believe if the story turned out to be true. Only 38 percent of them said they would be unmoved. The rest said their belief would increase. Now of course very few of this 62 percent said they would have to believe in Jesus' divinity if such a Roman file was discovered. As we noted in chapter 4, the "evidence" does not warrant *that* big a leap. Instead, the agnostics' overall median went from a 0 to a +1.[5] But they apparently thought the evidence would be relevant, and they indicated they would be swayed a bit by it.

Then how about the inactive believers? Seventy inactive Christian parents received the Attis version that challenged Jesus' existence. Their *pre*-test median equaled +3—indicating a strong belief in the divinity of Jesus, although less strong than the fundamentalists'. Afterward, 47 percent of these inactive believers said that if the Attis scroll were someday found and validated, their belief in Jesus nevertheless would *not* decrease. But the rest said it would. So both the agnostics and the inactive believers appear much more likely to be swayed by relevant evidence than the atheists and the high fundamentalists.[6]

Our third measure of dogmatism asked the parents if they could think of *any* event or evidence that would lead them to change their minds about the existence of the traditional Judeo-Christian God—a question they answered with a simple yes or no. As we saw in chapter 4 most (57 percent) of the atheists said no, nothing could lead them to believe. *All* of the high fundamentalists, who believe most strongly, said they could not possibly be budged. In turn, close to half (46 percent) of the agnostics said they could not conceive of any event or evidence that would lead them to believe. But 75 percent of the inactive believers, like 100 percent of the fundamentalists, said nothing could convince them this God did not exist. So a very solid majority of the believers indicated that their minds were permanently made up, no matter what happened. The nonbelievers showed greater openness to changing their minds.[7]

To summarize then, within the Manitoba parent sample the *agnostics'* and the *inactive believers'* scores on the DOG scale straddled those of the atheists. (See figure 9.1.) Both "in-between" groups—unlike most atheists and high fundamentalists—seemed willing to shift their beliefs about Jesus some if new evidence warranted it. The agnostics could think of things that would change their beliefs more often than atheists could, and so could the inactive believers compared with the fundamentalists. Overall agnostics proved the least closed-minded, the most flexible group over the three measures used, and at the other extreme no one could hold a candle to the high fundamentalists when it came to dogmatic certainty. If one supposes that the more extreme someone's religious views, pro-religion or con-, the more likely he is to be dogmatic, the data from this sample are *not* supportive. Instead, on two of the three measures, the *more religious* one is, the higher the dogmatism.

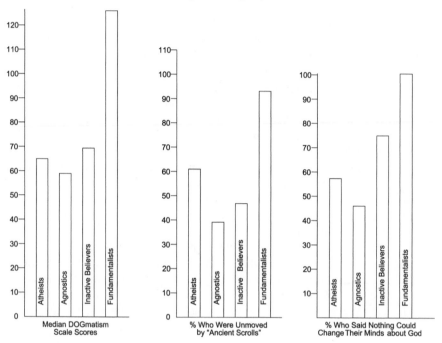

Figure 9.1

Dogmatism Scores among Four Subgroups of Manitoba Parents

ZEALOTRY

The Manitoba parents responded to several measures of zealotry. First they were asked what they would say to a teenager who was having doubts about her/his religious upbringing. Would atheists tell a teen with a religious background that religion was wrong (and, by implication, his/her parents)? We saw in chapter 5 that only 8 percent would do so. Even fewer (2 percent) of the agnostics would say this to a teen in this situation. Among the inactive believers, only 19 percent would tell a teen raised an atheist that atheism was wrong, but 88 percent of the high fundamentalists would.

Next the parents were asked if they would want the teen to end up believing what they believe. Thirty-five percent of the atheists said they would, but only 13 percent of the agnostics. However, 53 percent of the inactive believers wanted the teen to adopt their beliefs, as did a robust 96 percent of the high fundamentalists.

The "Questioning Teen" measure ended with the inquiry, "Would you try to lead them to share your beliefs?" Only 16 percent of the atheists said they would, but again the agnostics limbo'd under that with 8 percent. The inactive believers proved more pushy (42 percent), but no one topped the high fundamentalists for zealotry as a whopping 98 percent of them said they would try to convert the teen.

We also asked the parents if they wanted their children to have the same religious beliefs they had.

Reference to chapter 5 will show that 14 percent of the atheists said yes, they had; the rest of the atheists said they had wanted their children to make up their own minds. Only 7 percent of the agnostics, and 27 percent of the inactive believers replied that they wanted their offspring to have their own beliefs. But 94 percent of the high fundamentalists said they had raised their children to believe what they believed.

Finally, in our last measure of zealotry we asked nonbelievers if they would like atheism taught in public schools, and we similarly asked believers if they wanted a (fundamentalist) Christianity to become part of the curriculum. Zero percent of the atheists said they wanted their beliefs taught. (Ain't nobody squeezing under that!) Only 1 percent of the agnostics liked the idea. Meanwhile only 37 percent of the inactive Christians endorsed the teaching of fundamentalist Christianity to everyone's children. But 84 percent of the high fundamentalists liked that idea.[8]

These five sets of results converge into an easy and by now familiar summary (see figure 9.2). Agnostics have even less zealous passion burning in their breasts than atheists do. Those who believe in God but do not go to church show more proselytizing zeal than the nonbelievers do; but even so most of them have little interest in winning converts. Who does? Almost every one of the high fundamentalists.

RELIGIOUS ETHNOCENTRISM

We first discussed religious prejudice in chapter 6 in the context of the Religious Ethnocentrism scale. As noted then, this instrument was built primarily to measure such ethnocentrism among Christians, so one should question its validity among nonbelievers. We saw that the fifty-one Manitoba atheist parents had a median score of 38 on the scale, and the 45 Christian high fundamentalist parents racked up a stunning 103. How did the agnostics score? Higher than the atheists, with a median of 47, while the inactive believers posted a 53 that fell way, way short of the fundamentalists' average.[9]

The most interesting data on religious prejudice in chapter 6 were provided by the Thermometer measure that asked parents to evaluate ten different groups on a 0 to 100 scale. As we saw in table 6.1, the Manitoba atheists made very little distinction among the ten targets, giving most groups (including their own kind, Atheists) a middling 50, with the lowest rating, a nearby 30, going to Christian and Muslim fundamentalists. The *fundamentalist* parents in the sample discriminated much more, however, giving Christians and Believers in a traditional God median scores of 90, and Atheists a much lower 30.

The *agnostic* parents again snuck under the atheists, giving every group a median rating of 50 except Muslim fundamentalists, who got a 40. The *inactive believers* made slightly greater distinctions, giving Christians and Believers in a tra-

Figure 9.2

Zealotry Scores among Four Subgroups of Manitoba Parents

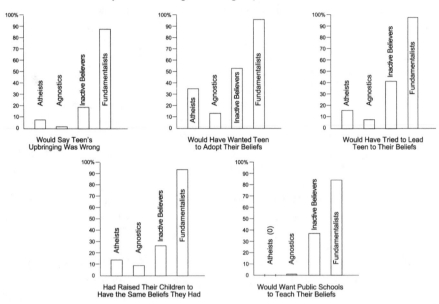

ditional God scores of 70 while everyone else got a 50. Note that the agnostic parents, like the atheists, gave their *own* group a neutral rating of 50. In contrast, the inactives rated people like themselves a 70, while the high fundamentalists liked their own kind even more with an 80 for Believers in a Traditional God and 90 for Christians. In short, the nonbeliever parents tended *not* to rate people like themselves higher or lower than others. But believers tended to think the world of people such as themselves. So among these Manitoba parents, the more religious one is, the more likely one is to pump up the in-group and be religiously ethnocentric.

OTHER VARIABLES

One can hardly miss the pattern in the results we have just considered. Agnostics almost always had the lowest scores on dogmatism, zealotry, and religious prejudice; the atheists usually placed second, while the inactive believers usually scored higher than any of the nonbelievers, and the high fundamentalists towered over everyone. Will this same order reappear when we consider the Manitoba parents' responses to chapter 7's "other variables": right-wing authoritarianism, racial/ethnic prejudice, hostility toward homosexuals, and opinions of evolution versus creation science?

Nope, not when it comes to right-wing authoritarianism. The atheist parents scored very low on the RWA scale (exhibit 7.5) with a median of 51, while the agnostics came in a full 20 points higher at 71. The gap between agnostics and inactive believers, who had a median of 81, was only half as wide, and the high fundamentalists, as always, soared above everyone else with a median of 135. But there is no curvilinear "dip" in these data; the farther a group gets from atheism, the higher their average level of right-wing authoritarianism.[10]

Does the same straightforward "positive" relationship appear between religiousness and racial/ethnic ethnocentrism? Yes. When the parent sample answered the Manitoba Ethnocentrism scale shown in exhibit 7.4, the atheists' median equaled 64. The agnostics came in at 72, just a hair under the inactive believers' 73. The fundamentalists had a median of 84—high but at least within the ballpark this time.[11]

When it came to hostility toward homosexuals, as measured by the scale shown in exhibit 7.3, the atheists averaged an extremely low 23, the agnostics a 32, the inactives a 33, and the high fundamentalists a 70. So again the atheists appear to be the least prejudiced, and the fundamentalists the most, with virtually no difference between the agnostics and the inactive believers.[12]

Finally, the parents also answered the twelve-item scale that measured belief in evolution versus creation science (exhibit 7.2). The atheists, as we noted in chapter 7, had a surprisingly high median of 38 on a scale that could range from 12 (pro-evolution) to 108 (pro–creation science). But that still fell well below the agnostics' median of 53, while the inactive believers landed squarely on the neutral point of the scale, a 60. The high fundamentalists, of course, strongly championed creation science (median of 95).[13]

These sundry results, summarized in figure 9.3, reveal a somewhat different pattern than we found on the measures of dogmatism, zealotry, and religious ethnocentrism. Most notably, the atheists always looked best by scoring lowest on these rather undesirable traits. The agnostics in turn proved indistinguishable from the inactive believers on our two measures of prejudice. But one beat pounded away in comparison after comparison: nobody topped the high fundamentalist, or usually even came close.

DISCUSSION

This book is titled *Atheists* but it mainly focuses on members of *atheists clubs* in America. Such persons command one's interest because they are having such a dramatic impact on their society through the courts. But are they representative of the much larger number of less active atheists? Probably not, but we have no information about less active atheist Americans in our investigations. We do have some data from presumably "ordinary" atheists in a rather ordinary collection of Canadian adults, and in previous chapters we have compared them with highly fundamentalist persons in that same sample. These groups differed markedly on all of our measures.

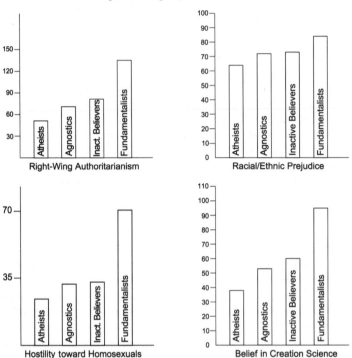

Figure 9.3

Authoritarianism, Prejudice, and Belief in Creation Science Scores
among Four Subgroups of Manitoba Parents

Now we have worked two other groups into the picture: agnostics, and those who say they believe in God and belong to a religion but do not go to church.

What say the agnostics? Two sets of results emerged. First, when it comes to dogmatism, zealotry, and religious ethnocentrism, the agnostic parents almost always scored *lower* than everyone else, including their fellow nonbelievers, the atheists (see figures 9.1 and 9.2). This makes sense if you suppose that agnostics have a two-sided outlook on such matters. What is the point of being dogmatic, zealous, and stand-offish about something you frankly do not know? But second, on our measures of authoritarianism, prejudice, and belief in creation science, the atheists brought in the lowest scores. Sometimes, in fact, the agnostics barely scooted under the inactive believers.

Why did the agnostics score so relatively high in these latter regards? Well, a collection of self-described agnostics, more so than atheists, probably includes some people whose "I don't know" stand regarding God has resulted, not from consideration of arguments and evidence for a deity, but rather from a decided lack of interest in religion. Such indifference would certainly help lower the agnostics' scores on dogmatism, zealotry, and religious ethnocentrism, but when it came to authoritarianism and prejudice, these more ordinary people—compared with atheists—would have a more ordinary range of scores, which would raise the agnostics' averages above the atheists'. Indifference about religion might also have raised the agnostics' attitudes toward creation science closer to the neutral point.

Then let us turn our attention to the inactive believers, where indifference may run rampant. We found that the inactives had a bit more religious upbringing than the agnostics did—enough to produce a belief in God at least. And their theism shows—if it requires demonstration—that believing in God does not automatically make one highly dogmatic, zealous, intolerant, authoritarian, and prejudiced. But why do the inactive believers believe in God, given how closely they resembled the nonbelievers on many of our measures? Many fundamentalists might say the inactives *do not really* believe, for if they did they would be active. And, in fact, about half of the inactives doubt that God will judge them someday. But most of them do believe in an eternal deity that is all-good, all-loving, and hears our prayers. So it is a comforting package of beliefs, and they get to sleep in on Sundays to boot. But it strikes at the heart of organized religion. The odds are slim that the children of inactives will go to church, and they may not even carry on their parents' qualified belief in God.[14]

Why had the inactive believers found going to church unrewarding? They said they disliked the way religious people sometimes pressured others to believe what they believe. They disliked the intolerance some religious people showed, both toward other religions and toward homosexuals. They observed that faith can make people blind. But we have seen that the high fundamentalists lead the league in evangelizing, intolerance, and dogmatism. The inactives also said they had been turned off by the hypocrisy they had seen among "the holy," and we recall from the introduction that this was the biggest reason another sample of Manitoba parents gave for not passing along the family religion to their children. So the high fundamentalists may have made some unintended conversions here, turning believers into inactives.

FILLING THE GAPS: REGULAR ATTENDERS AND MODESTLY ACTIVE BELIEVERS

The generally large gaps in our data between the inactive believers and the high fundamentalists testifies to the peculiarity of the latter, who after all were not culled to represent the "average religious person," but to provide a comparison group as extremely religious as the atheists were extremely nonreligious. Recall from chapter 1 that these fifty-one high fundamentalists scored a good twenty points higher on the Religious Fundamentalism scale than our average Canadian fundamentalist Protestant does.

So what is the more ordinary "religious person" like—say the one who attends services most weeks but is not a high fundamentalist? Well most (59 percent) of the parents said they do not go to church at all, but a little over two hundred of the 836 parents reported they attended services at least three times per month. If we set aside the fifty-one high fundamentalists whom we have already analyzed up, down, and sideways, we are left with 155 other regular churchgoers who did not score so highly on the Religious Fundamentalism scale.

They are, as expected, mostly women (58 percent), the usual forty-eight years old on the average, and they went to school for a median thirteen years. Eighty-five percent of their responses to the seven questions about the traditional God were affirmative (see table 9.1). Their Doubts scale scores had a median of 38, and their Religious Emphasis answers averaged 26. Their median DOGmatism score came in at 91; 60 percent of those who got the Attis version of the ancient scrolls experiment said they would be unmoved by the new evidence; 88 percent said nothing could change their minds about the existence of the traditional God. Thirty-seven percent of them would tell a questioning teen raised an atheist that his/her upbringing was wrong; 75 percent would want this teen to eventually adopt their beliefs; and 73 percent said they would try to lead a teen in that direction. Sixty-six percent said they raised their children to have the same religious beliefs they had and 51 percent said they would favor a law requiring the teaching of Christianity in public schools. Their median score on the Religious Ethnocentrism scale equaled 64; they gave their highest Thermometer ratings to Christians and believers in a traditional God (80) and their lowest ratings (40) to atheists, for an in-group versus out-group difference of forty points. Their median RWA scale score was 98; that on the Manitoba Ethnocentrism scale equaled 75; their hostility toward homosexuals averaged 46; while their beliefs about evolution favored creation science (68).[15]

Table 9.1 lets us compare at a glance these 155 regular church attenders with the fifty-one high fundamentalists who join them at services. The high fundamentalists really are high, being much firmer believers, substantially more dogmatic, and especially more zealous and proselytizing. They also are more religiously ethnocentric, authoritarian, and prejudiced. But still, the regular church attenders have higher scores on almost all these variables than the inactive believers who believe but never go to church. They may not post the extreme scores of the high fundamentalists, but it does seem that going to church regularly is associated with all the variables in our study—and unhappily so in most cases.

Is this connection really there? Let's look at the group we have skipped over thus far, the (119) "Modestly Active Believers" who go to church once or twice a month. If you run your finger down their column in table 9.1, you will see that— measure for measure—they almost always score somewhere between those who believe but never go to church, and those who believe and go regularly.[16]

Table 9.1 thus appears to reveal a provocative truth. If you ask a large bunch of rather ordinary middle-aged persons all sorts of questions about religion, such as their background, what they believe, how they see other people, and what they would do in various situations, an unmistakable trend jumps out of the data. Throw in measures of authoritarianism, dogmatism, zealotry, and prejudice, and the same trend reappears. The scores usually march steadily along from atheists to high fundamentalists. Most of the "mis-steps" one finds pile up in the atheists' dogmatism and proselytizing

Table 9.1
Scores on Various Dimensions of Manitoba Parents, Broken Down by Religious Groupings

Variable	Atheists	Agnostics	Inactive Believers	Modestly Active Believers	Regular Church Attenders	Very High Funda- mentalists
Sample Size[a]	N = 51	N = 183	N = 199	N = 119	N = 155	N = 51
Demographics: Gender (% Female)	39%	46%	57%	56%	58%	51%
Median Age	48	48	48	47	48	48
Median Yrs of Education	15	14	12	13	13	13
% "Yes," 7 Attributes of God	1%	15%	74%	82%	85%	98%
Median Religious Doubts	73	60	47	44	38	18
Median Religious Emphasis	8	10	17	21	26	37
Median Dogmatism	65	58	69	73	91	126
Ancient Scrolls: % Unchanged Belief[b]	64%	38%	47%	58%	60%	93%
Nothing Can Change Belief about God[b]	57%	46%	75%	84%	88%	100%
Tell Questioning Teen Beliefs Wrong[b]	8%	2%	19%	12%	37%	88%
Want Teen to Have Their Beliefs[b]	35%	13%	53%	69%	75%	96%
Would Try to Convert Teen[b]	16%	8%	42%	70%	73%	98%
Raised Children to Have Same Beliefs	14%	7%	27%	50%	66%	94%
Favor Law Teaching Beliefs in School[b]	0%	1%	37%	42%	51%	84%
Median Religious Ethnocentrism	38	47	53	61	64	103
"Thermometer:" Highest Minus Lowest Rank	20	10	20	30	40	60
Median Right-Wing Authoritarianism	51	71	81	93	98	135
Median Manitoba Ethnocentrism	64	72	73	80	75	84
Median Hostility toward Homosexuals	23	32	33	40	46	70
Median Belief in Creation Science	38	53	60	64	68	95

[a]Missing from this analysis are respondents who did not answer the question about belief in God, or the question about church attendance, or the particular variable being considered.

[b]For these variables, the values for the atheists and agnostics represent the responses to opposite versions of the questions asked theists/Christians. Thus nonbelievers were asked, in the Ancient Scrolls question, if archaeological evidence *supporting* the Gospels would affect their belief that Jesus was not the son of God. In the "Convince" question, they were asked if anything could convince them the traditional God *exists*. In the "Questioning Teen" questions they were asked how they would respond to a teen *raised in Christianity*. In the Favor Law Teaching Beliefs in School question, they were asked if they would like a law forcing public schools to teach God does *not* exist.

scores, which we saw are relatively high for nonbelievers. (But see note 9.) Look at the scores of the four groups of theists. One finds a numbing progression, variable after variable. There are $(17 \times 5 =)$ eighty-five "steps" in these data, and seventy-five of them form flights of stairs all heading in the same direction.

Is this really that surprising? Nonbelievers are hardly likely to proclaim the attributes of God, they will naturally have tons of religious doubts, and they will tend to come from nonreligious families. Will not the activity level among believers also reflect these factors? But what about the personality traits and prejudice? However ambiguous the causal direction of these relationships, the associations themselves could hardly be clearer. It is almost as if a law had been passed saying that as religiosity ranges from 0 to 100, so also will dogmatism, zealotry, authoritarianism, and prejudice generally increase.

If we pass this by too quickly, saying "Naturally," we shortchange the possibility that it could be otherwise. Could not religiousness, in principle, be solidly connected to being open-minded, unassuming and retiring, freedom-loving, and charitable toward all? But it is not; it is just the opposite in this study. Nonbelievers, including the atheists, usually proved less dogmatic, less zealous, less authoritarian, and less prejudiced than any of the believer groups, even the relatively low-scoring inactive believers. Is that not provocative?

We hasten to add three things in closing. First, as you probably noticed, we are making value judgments about being dogmatic, zealous, authoritarian, and so on. Someone could argue that at times these might be desirable traits. But in the long run, in most situations, they seem to us quite destructive, and if we are wrong about that, we need to be enlightened. Second, all of these findings are *group* findings, and many individuals in our samples looked quite different from their group's average. Finally, if you find all of this complete nonsense, if you think we have asked the wrong questions or biased the study in a dozen ways or wildly misinterpreted the evidence, matters can still be redeemed. This study can be repeated and checked out and improved upon by anyone in our business. Which we hope is the business of finding out the truth, no matter what it is.

NOTES

1. All of these differences are statistically significant from each other. That is, the atheists' disbelief in the traditional God is significantly greater than the agnostics', and the fundamentalists' belief in that deity is significantly greater than the inactive believers'.

2. The mean Doubts score for the four groups are 69.9 for the atheists, 58.7 for the agnostics, 49.1 for the inactive believers, and 21.3 for the fundamentalists. All of these means are significantly different from one another.

3. The mean Religious Emphasis score for the groups proceeded as follows: 9.8 for the atheists, 13.1 for the agnostics, 18.8 for the inactive believers, and 33.0 for the fundamentalists. All of these means are significantly different from one another.

4. As sometimes happens with different measures of central tendency, the *means* of the

scores on the Dogmatism scale paint a somewhat different picture than the medians do. The atheists' mean equaled 59.4, and the agnostics' mean was higher, at 61.4. The inactive believers punched up a 69.6, and the fundamentalists posted a robust 124.9. The atheists' and agnostics' means are not significantly different (t = 0.57; t > 0.50). All other comparisons are significantly different.

5. Converting the -4 to +4 scale to a 1 to 9 format, where "neutral" equals 5, the means for the agnostics shifted from a pretest 4.82 to a posttest 6.15, which is statistically significant beyond the 0.001 level.

6. The difference between the agnostics (38 percent) and the inactive believers (47 percent) is not statistically significant (t = 1.33; p > .20). All other differences are significant.

7. The difference between the atheists' and the agnostics' scores is not statistically significant (t = 1.19; p > .25). All other differences are significant.

8. The fundamentalists' score is always significantly higher than any other group's on all five measures of zealotry. Beyond that, the atheists and agnostics are only significantly different on the "Want teen to believe what you believe" question, and the inactive believers are almost always significantly more zealous than the agnostics and the atheists.

9. The "curvilinear dip" does not mean the differences between atheists and agnostics were *statistically significant*. In fact, they seldom were. The mean Religious Ethnocentrism score for the atheists was 38.8, while the agnostics posted a 47.6. The inactive believers had a 52.8 while the high fundamentalists' mean equaled 101.3. The latter was significantly higher than any of the others. The atheists' mean was significantly lower than the inactive believers, but not that of the agnostics (t = 1.66; p < .10).

10. The means came in at 53.1, 71.1, 80.8, and 133.8. All of these are significantly different from the others.

11. The means were 61.5, 73.7, 73.4, and 81.2. The tiny (and inverted) difference between the agnostics' and inactives' means is not statistically significant, but all the others are.

12. Here the means ran 28.1, 35.0, 36.1, and 68.3. Again, the wisp of a difference between the agnostics and the inactive believers does not even approach statistical significance, but the other means are all significantly different from one another.

13. The means spaced themselves out at 38.4, 48.6, 61.4, and 91.2. All are significantly different from the others.

14. The 199 inactive parents came from 158 different families. So in 41 (199 minus 158) families both parents were inactive believers, and predictably almost none of their children ever went to church. The other 117 families had just one parent who was an inactive believer. Typically the *other* parent also never went to church, usually because he flat-out did not belong to any religion. But 32 students had one parent who practiced the family religion and another who said he belonged to that religion but did not go to church. How many of those 32 students do you think went to church themselves? Only 12, and 11 of them only went once or twice a month. So a family may be "Catholic" and one of the parents may go to mass on Sunday. But if the other parent does not, neither usually will their children by the time they are young adults.

15. The means which accompany the medians for the regular churchgoers are as follows—Doubts: 40.9; Religious Emphasis: 24.0; Dogmatism: 84.6; Religious Ethnocentrism: 64.5; RWA: 96.5; Manitoba Ethnocentrism: 77.2; Attitudes toward Homosexuals: 45.4; belief in Creation Science: 68.6. These means are always significantly lower than those for the 51 fundamentalists, and with only one exception (the Manitoba Ethnocentrism scale) significantly different from those of the 199 Manitoba inactive believers.

16. Here are the means for the 119 modestly active believers—Doubts: 46.4; Religious Emphasis: 21.4; Dogmatism: 75.2; Religious Ethnocentrism: 60.0; RWA: 92.7; Manitoba Ethnocentrism: 79.7; Attitudes toward Homosexuals: 41.9; belief in Creation Science: 66.4. Thanks to good sample sizes, most of these means are significantly different from the corresponding values of the inactive believers *and* those of the regular churchgoers.

CHAPTER 10

RESPONSES FROM MEMBERS OF THE ATHEIST ORGANIZATIONS WE SURVEYED

The authors and Prometheus Books felt that this book would be enriched by comments from the American atheists clubs whose members had participated in the study. Accordingly we sent Chris Lindstrom the manuscript pages for everything through chapter 8 in the fall of 2004 (chapter 9 was in preparation), and asked her to forward them to the clubs along with our request for feedback. Many of the clubs obliged, and here are the eight responses we received, in the order in which they arrived.[1]

1. CHRIS LINDSTROM, FORMER SECRETARY OF ATHEISTS OF SILICON VALLEY AND FOUNDER OF THE GARRISON-MARTINEAU PROJECT (WWW.GARRISON-MARTINEAU.COM)[2]

First of all, I wanted to thank Dr. Altemeyer and Dr. Hunsberger for taking what I hope will be the first small step to answering some intriguing questions. I'm looking forward to the day when I can cruise the library and see a book titled *The Varieties of the Nonreligious Experience* next to William James's classic. Second, I just wanted to make a quick note about the return rate. I actually think that the return rate is larger than the 50% reported because we know that the mailing lists of our local clubs are not mutually exclusive. While I personally eliminated the duplicates from the lists of the three atheist organizations, the three humanist organizations made independent mailings. Additionally, while the professors mention the possibility that some more moderate atheists and humanists did not fill out the survey, these are likely balanced by those who told me that the survey was not "atheist enough" for them!

When the results came in, we had a lively discussion about them at our local group meeting. We laughed when told that the researchers were surprised that we were—in my words "mostly male and mostly 60." One gentleman told me that from now on he is reporting his age as "mostly 60." (I noticed he declined to identify his gender as "mostly male.") I am glad to see these results published if only to diminish long-standing cultural stereotypes of atheists as hedonistic teenage rebels. Our leadership has worried about our age demographic and talked about what it means for years, but I think the best explanation is economic. With both parents working and Little League games to attend, who has time for social change work? Although I am interested in seeing more age diversity among our ranks, I'm grateful for all of the volunteer retirees who do a lot of the organizational heavy lifting (and welcome any potential volunteers—of any age—who might be reading this now!).

We were also unsurprised to find that the professors thought us dogmatic—we had, after all, filled out the survey and we could see where it was headed—but my group definitely rejected the label. I'm inclined to agree with them. The professors used three different measures to determine dogmatism: asking if people could imagine something that would change their mind, the Roman file and the "DOG scale." Of these three, two have serious weaknesses. What would change your mind? If we were to ask people what data might change their mind about the correlation between smoking and cancer, we might think that people who could not devise some experiment as lacking a good science education. However, when faced with the Ineffable, Invisible, and Indescribable, one should perhaps cut the respondents some slack. The half of us who could think of something that would convince us god existed proposed that the half of us who could not showed a "serious lack of imagination" but not dogmatism. (One man said he thought $10 million would be enough to convince him, but that regular church attendance would cost extra!) The Roman file. The story about the Roman file describes scientifically validated ancient parchments which verified Jesus' life and miracles. However, respondents were not asked if this new file would modify their views about the historicity of the Gospels but rather about whether Jesus was divine and the son of God. This question essentially assumes that respondents share a common assumption that if the miracles were actually observed Jesus would be the Son of God. It is probably safe to say that this assumption is not likely to be shared by many of our atheist and humanist members who are commonly skeptical of modern-day psychics and spoon benders, in spite of the many apparent eyewitnesses. If we throw out these two measures, we are left with the DOG scale on which the atheists had a mean score of 85.3, which is somewhat higher than the mean score from the parents of introductory psychology students at the University of Manitoba (75) but much lower than the religious fundamentalists (100). It could be that the difference between the parent sample and our responses is due primarily to cultural and age differences. I do not think that on the basis of the survey it is possible to say whether or not our membership is dogmatic. I do know that while it can be difficult to stop an atheist once she has begun an impassioned treatise, we are also genuinely inquisitive individuals. I would like to see future surveys asking a broader range of questions about our willingness to consider new evidence in a range of areas: political, scientific, economic, health-related, etc.

Finally, I was absolutely astounded to see our high ethnocentrism scores. We seem to have outdone even the fundamentalist Christians in breaking off our arms to pat ourselves on the back. The Canadian Christian fundamentalists ranked themselves 54.4 points higher than atheists on the favorability scale. We ranked ourselves a whopping 72.7 points higher than them! When I suggested to my group that we might be a tad prejudiced, they disagreed, but one gentleman in the back who kept interrupting to explain why he was justified in saying that he would always prefer a nonreligious gardener made me think there was some truth to it. I suppose that these results should not have surprised me since I have been to enough atheist meetings and heard enough grousing about religious people, but in my defense, I didn't really think that deep down my fellow atheists actually believed what they were saying. Weren't they just venting? Or saying something outrageous just to get a word in edgewise?

Part of my confusion lay in my conviction that most of my fellow atheists were, like myself, raised in strongly religious families with many family members remaining strongly religious. In other words, I thought that most of my colleagues were "recovering fundamentalists" who, while angry, would never really think of their own relatives as stupid or worse! However, according to the survey, more than 30% of us had at least one parent who was an atheist or an agnostic and most were raised in only nominally religious homes. Under the circumstances, I guess that the chasm between our own experiences and those of Christians combined with our anger at how easily atheist concerns are ignored in the political arena just proved too much for us. I am reminded of an atheist friend of mine who told me once that she spends about 50% of her time trying to get other atheists to understand that not all Christians are "hateful fundamentalists" and the other 50% of her time dealing with "hateful fundamentalists." Obviously, if we atheists and Humanists desire to live in a world where we are judged as individuals rather than on stereotypes about our group, we should be leading the way by doing the same for others. I currently run an organization that facilitates face-to-face small group dialogue between believers and nonbelievers because I believe it is a piece of the puzzle, a way to enable people to see and be seen as human beings and reduce misperceptions and stereotypes which exist on both sides. And besides, it seemed to work for the Christians and the Jews. They went from talking about a "Christian" culture to a "Judeo-Christian culture." Maybe someday Pat Robertson's successor will be talking about our "Enlightenment-Judeo-Christian" culture or even a "Humanist-Judeo-Christian culture"!

One of the more interesting results to come out of this survey and the similar survey of college students documented in Amazing Conversions is that non-believers do not only differ quantitatively in terms of doubt, but also qualitatively. We experience entirely different kinds of doubt. The doubt category that ranked highest for us was "Religious teachings often did not make sense; they seemed contradictory or unbelievable." How is it possible that people who had crossed the Red Sea and eaten manna from heaven built a golden calf just because their leader was a few hours late returning from his appointment with the Almighty? Why was genocide OK for King Saul but not Hitler? Why is Jesus supposed to be perfect and yet at the same time cursing a fig tree, lying to the mother of a dead girl and calling a Samaritan woman a dog? For believers, on the other hand, this same category hardly registered; instead they admitted to struggling with doubt regarding bereavement and life meaning. I overheard a conversation at one of my sponsored dialogues recently that highlighted our different questions. The group included two atheists, an evangelical Christian and a liberal believer whose spirituality was his own but had a lot in common with Eastern mysticism. At one point, the liberal believer said, "You know, I feel like I have a lot in common with the Christian because I can relate to the questions he was asking, 'What is the meaning of my life?' Do you atheists even ask that question?" One of the atheists responded by explaining that the question didn't really make sense to him. For instance, if he discovered that his meaning/destiny in life was to save someone from a burning building, what should he then do? Should he hang out in front of the building waiting for his big day of destiny? Or should he assume it would happen by serendipity and just go about life as he always did? These two people were obviously talking on different levels—even as they used the same vocabulary! Atheists do feel their lives have meaning (to themselves and others) in the here and now, but don't feel or understand cosmic yearnings for something deeper. I find it fascinating that where people end up to a large extent depends on the questions one asks. I have no idea why atheists do not have burning questions about life meaning. I likewise have no idea why believers don't seem to experience burning questions about floating axe heads and parting seas. However, these differences seem to indicate potential areas of future research.

I sold the survey to the local leadership as a way for us to learn something about ourselves and perhaps even get ideas about how to attract the many millions of other people who are already atheists to our cause. The good news is that I was mistaken about who is interested in joining our groups. I thought our target market was the "amazing apostates"—that 1% of people who are raised in strong religious backgrounds and yet abandon religion—which would be a pretty difficult group to target in terms of a direct mailing. Instead, our membership is simply a portion of the much larger 14% of the American population who are non-religious (City University of New York Religious Self Identification Study 2000). Our opportunities are much expanded. We are literally surrounded by potential allies! I've met quite a few fellow nonbelievers who are already active at work on causes we also care about: civil liberties, media accountability, peace and justice, reproductive choice, environmental stewardship and many more. I do not know if this larger group of nonbelievers will join our organizations, but if we work alongside them, building friendships, who knows what we can accomplish.

2. BRAD SMITH, MEMBER, SECULAR HUMANISTS OF THE EAST BAY (WWW.EASTBAYHUMANISTS.ORG), ADJUNCT PROFESSOR, UNIVERSITY OF SAN FRANCISCO

"But first, let's have some fun and tear this study to pieces, limb by limb."

As a methodologist, it's hard for me to imagine a better approach than this. It's a wonderful and appropriate way to begin and I believe the authors cover the various methodological challenges that could be raised against their study in an effective and understandable way. I found the results of the study fascinating and very much enjoyed the accessible and inviting way in which it was written.

I was a little concerned about the comparisons made between the 253 Bay Area respondents and the 28 respondents from Alabama or Idaho. With only 28 respondents from Alabama or Idaho, it's hard for me to get my head around what the comparison reveals about atheists in the United States (or in Alabama or Idaho for that matter). If asked, I believe I would have recommended not using the data from Alabama or Idaho.

I'm sure the scale was defined and described earlier in the book, but a reminder that the RWA scale is the Right-Wing Authoritarianism scale would be helpful to those who, even with the entire book in hand, may skip to the final chapter to see how it all turns out.[3]

It could easily just be me, but for whatever it's worth, I had trouble making the journey from the results of the survey to the ten predictions about ordinary American atheists. I did feel "repeatedly clapped on the back," which was strange because the high level of dogmatism for atheists was certainly among the more intriguing, but less flattering, findings. I could easily imagine this description holding up on a broader survey that included both believers and non-believers.

These are minor points. I'm looking forward to reading the entire book when it's released.

3. LARRY HICOK, COORDINATOR, EAST BAY ATHEISTS (WWW.EASTBAYATHEISTS.ORG)

As an atheist for over forty years, I stopped taking this survey when I saw the second question. An atheist is here defined as someone who "believe(s)" God does not exist. According to the definition supplied by the survey, I am not an atheist. I am not really an agnostic either, since I certainly disbelieve (reject as false the concept that) there is a God.

The problem centers on the use of the term "belief." The "beliefs" of atheists are counterpoised to the beliefs of theists. Agnostics are presented as the rational middle, lacking beliefs either way. I find this insulting. I would maintain that atheism is simply a logical conclusion based on the lack of scientific evidence to the contrary.

The atheist movement for the last several years has been reexamining the propriety of traditional uses of "belief." Belief implies conviction, commonly accompanied by faith, in direct opposition to conclusions based on evidence and solid logic. Although it lacks any scientific certainty, it implies absolute certainty, while science sees nothing as absolutely certain.

In our culture, the irrational traits noted above best describe a "Believer." Why, then, should opinions, logical conclusions demanded by evidence, and admittedly subjective taste preferences, be put on the same level as what are most accurately referred to as beliefs, when their essence is that they lack those very qualities most associated with belief? Is this not because our Judeo-Christian culture is so defined by belief that it does not even recognize knowledge as an entirely different category?

Getting back to the survey's definition of an atheist as someone who "believes" God does not exist, this to me implies a disillusioned theist who has felt betrayed by God, and therefore believes He does not exist. This is the definition of an atheist supplied by the theist media, typically depicted by Mel Gibson in "Signs." It is by no means mine.

Bias is again evinced in the survey's examination of the level of dogmatism in the sampled atheists. An ancient Roman "file" documenting the truths of Christ is found. It contains eyewitness accounts of miracles. Surely such ancient anecdotal accounts from a superstitious people do not rise to the level of evidence accepted by science. Yet atheists who were not swayed by this file were considered dogmatic.

Again atheists are portrayed as dogmatic because for many there are no "conceivable events or evidence that would lead (them) to believe." I submit that if the Christian God were to appear in person throughout the world, and perform miracles all the while, virtually all atheists would conclude that he exists. (I suspect few would embrace him, however, as he is a horrible tyrant.) To ask us if such an event is "conceivable" implies for many that it has at least some level of possibility. If the authors truly wanted to measure dogmatism, they should have generated a scenario in which scientifically valid evidence, including repeatability, was presented, instead of this nebulous concoction.

The argument could be made that these questions were the reverse of those asked theists to determine their level of dogmatism. Theism is not rational, but emotional; it flows from ancient myths, handed down as memes, not from repeatable evidence. Finding a common ground on which to judge the characteristics of both would be a challenge. The answer is certainly not found in reversing the scenarios used for theists.

The remainder of the survey portrayed atheists fairly accurately, in my opinion. The authors are to be commended for at least attempting this study, but my experience with atheists is that they are only "dogmatic" about relying on solid evidence and logic. Nothing in this survey contradicts that, regardless of the opinions of the authors.

4. ARTHUR M. JACKSON, PRESIDENT, HUMANIST COMMUNITY

I want to thank the authors for focusing their efforts to provide a better understanding of atheists as human beings. However, I'm convinced that the approach used here has some grave errors. I'm not able to state these reservations clearly and up to this point haven't had the motivation to clarify these errors.

Because atheists are often as involved in theism as Christians and Jews I think it's a mistake to call them non-believers. In fact I don't think there are any "non-believers." Everyone bases their life and their choices on their beliefs. So they must have beliefs.

I am an atheist, but my moral system is based on my humanism which forms my belief system; i.e., my religion. A primary goal of my life was to find a religion that was not incongruent with a scientific view of the universe. I see Humanism as having the potential to do that.

I think your below questions about the extent to which logic and science bring an atheist happiness, joy, and comfort are seminal and point out an area of current deficiency among atheists. The fact that each of the below questions was not answered with a 6 demonstrates how traditional religions have not only misled their converts, but has helped to lead science and those who seek to follow its approach astray.

. . . When Descartes' error is corrected and modern individuals realize that the meaning of their life is laid down in their genes as a result of evolution, not imposed by supernatural agencies we then have a basis to move ethics into the scientific domain and use empirical study to demonstrate how each person can indeed experience a life of happiness, joy, and comfort. My life's goal has been to promote that step and I share my results on my web page www.arthurmjackson.com/wpre.html.

As a result of these interests I am very active in the Humanist Community in Silicon Valley and in that way was introduced to your questionnaire.

Although over all I think your project was well done, it seems to me that some of the assumptions in your DOG scale are off-base. Most persons become atheists because they rejected dogmatism and tried to find the truth behind all the conflicting religious claims. To assume that questioning "scientifically validated ancient parchments" based on "eye-witness confirmation of the miracles reported in the Gospels, which painstaking examination could not discredit" makes one dogmatic seems to me a gross misinterpretation of the evaluation a critical thinker would bring to this question. A valid report of claims does not make the claims true.

I won't quibble with your conclusion that "dogmatism is not incompatible with disbelief," since I've been around dogmatic atheists much of my life. However, I don't believe your questionnaire supports that conclusion.

Thanks for your effort to shed some light on the nature of atheists. I hope these efforts will encourage others to pursue the path you have laid out.

5. DAVID FITZGERALD, STEERING COMMITTEE MEMBER, SAN FRANCISCO ATHEISTS (WWW.SFATHEISTS.COM)

I want to first say how much I appreciate Prof. Altemeyer and Prof. Hunsberger for deciding that Atheist and Agnostic groups were worthy of study and for creating the survey. I found it very interesting reading. I'd also like to offer a word or two in the Atheist/Agnostic community's defense concerning the measures used to obtain the Dogmatism and Ethnocentrism scores.

The first measure I found problematic was the "Roman File" exercise. On the face of it, this postulated scenario might sound reasonable, but it suffers from the assumption that historical documentation is the major hurdle in accepting the divinity of Jesus. This is a topic near and dear to me, as I have spent the last 4 years researching the Historical Jesus question and am currently writing a book on the subject. Of course the total lack of contemporary accounts of Christ is a serious unanswered problem for Christian apologists, but it is far from the only one: there is also the matter of parallels to the numerous pagan mystery faith saviors of the time. Also, there are the discernable borrowings from sources such as the Old Testament, Greek and Roman literature, and historians such as Josephus, and more. There is also the clear evolution of the figure of Christ and of Christologies. And there is the multitude of discrepancies between the gospel accounts themselves, their late creation, questionable authorship, general reliability, etc. These are serious considerations that need to be addressed, and they are merely connected to the historicity of Christ, to say nothing of any claims of divinity, which is freighted with still more layers of difficulties!

Which takes us to the third measure: "What would be required for you to believe in the 'traditional' God?" This presumes that it's even possible to agree on, and make sense of, the many contradictory traditional conceptions of God, all of which collapse under their own logical shortcomings. The paradoxical Trinity doctrine, the problem of Evil, the logic pitfalls of God's omnipotence, omniscience, and omni benevolence, etc, etc. all bring to mind the reply of the Marquis La Place, when Napoleon asked him why he said so much about the Universe, but nothing about its Creator? "Sire, I had no need for that hypothesis."

If dogmatism is by definition the vigorous holding of an opinion (often unwarranted) without allowing any evidence to the contrary to sway it, then those who upon examination recognize the implausibilities and impossibilities of the two measures surely aren't guilty of being dogmatic!

Dogmatism is predicated on the prejudicial unwillingness to consider the evidence that challenges one's core beliefs. As your results showed, Atheists simply can't believe what does not make sense. Rejecting the scenarios upon examination of the question isn't the same as refusing to consider the question outright!

Now, that said, I'm sure we all know from personal experience that Atheists can indeed be dogmatic in the unwillingness to consider new evidence, but I think the vast majority of Atheists and Agnostics came to that position through a process of examining evidence. I suggest it would be interesting to study the ways in which dogmatism differs between believers and nonbelievers.

Similarly, I'd like to offer some possible mitigating factors for our Ethnocentrism index on Overall Group Attitudes. I question whether we can really determine prejudice from our reaction to any given group. Reaction to individuals is not the same as reaction to the group in question as a whole. As individuals, fundamentalists can be some of the loveliest people; many Atheists (myself included) have beloved fundamentalist friends and relatives. I love the quote I heard from Ellen

Johnson of American Atheists: "Religion makes good people better and bad people worse." With that in mind, Fundamentalists as a whole and the fundamentalist political agenda are seen unfavorably and arguably with good reason. But this is not from an unreasonable a priori prejudice.

I hope that this is helpful. Thanks again and I hope that more studies of free-thinkers takes place in the future!

6. BILL JACOBSEN, EXECUTIVE DIRECTOR, HUMANIST COMMUNITY (WWW.HUMANISTS.ORG)

In trying to get at what motivates people in the Humanist Community in Palo Alto, I don't think it's helpful to pose questions that assume all of them are in rebellion against Christianity or are heavily invested in denying the existence of some kind of deity. Some of us, at least, define ourselves in terms other than a mere negation of the orthodox or fundamentalist versions of Christianity. We'd be formulating our stance and acting on it, even if suddenly all supernaturalists disappeared. As for how we'd relate to moderates and liberals who aren't true believers—and now I speak for myself—I'd look upon them as allies to the extent they share my positive concerns.

Also, I feel it's a trap if Humanists fail to find affirmative equivalents to ideas that are so easily expressed in a negative manner. So instead of referring to a meaningless and indifferent cosmos, I talk about how I create my own meanings and purposes as I inscribe who I am on the blank pages of a book called My Life. And rather than discuss the fallibility of the Bible or deny miracles, I merely refer to the single standard that any historian must abide by. Nor do I need to deny there's cheese on the moon or that there's evidence for a benign all powerful deity, given all the needless suffering of innocents in the real world—I live in a world where such questions don't even arise.

Below I offer my answers to nine useful questions that bring out more clearly what makes me tick as a human being. I'd like to see how my colleagues of varied religious persuasions would respond to them.

Nine Questions that Reveal the Humanist as Ethicist, Activist, and Detective: Wisdom, Foresight, and Curiosity are the Driving Forces in My Humanism

A. The Humanist as Ethicist: Wisdom Calls Forth Humane Attitudes

Let's face it, not all virtues are wholesome. Empathy can degenerate into sentimentality, indignation can lead to self-righteousness, and reverence can foster superstition. Accordingly, I use adjectives that reduce the chances of "virtue-toxicity." That's why I favor a "realistic" empathy, a "humble" indignation, and a "discerning" reverence.

1. Who Matters? I bear the genes of animals that survived using violence, self-deception, guile, and deceit. To compensate for this, I give policy priorities to those

who need my compassion. I have in mind the vulnerables—the discriminated against, the poor, and the handicapped. I am a TAB, the temporarily able-bodied, able-minded, socially favored, and affluent. I also think of the invisibles—those distant in space and time (future generations) I'll never see. To avoid an unrealistic sentimentality, my empathy must be rooted in pragmatism. Hence I call for a "realistic empathy."

2. What Matters? I look to basic emotions that supplement compassion. At an early age healthy children develop a sense of fairness and an aversion to brutality, intimidation, and teasing. Nowadays I understand how governments and the legal systems operate during times of war and rightly hearken back to this fundamental urge to eliminate injustice and torture. The danger of becoming self-righteous lurks in the background. Therefore my indignation at inhumane and unjust actions must be tempered by self-examination and by laughing at my own pretensions and double standards. I'm a supreme rationalizer, ready to see the speck in the eye of my opponent, but unable to perceive the lumberyard in my own eye. Hence I call for a "humble indignation."

3. What Do I Revere? I refer not to piety, but to a sense of something greater than this bag of bones and muscles I call myself. Some religionists who've been enraptured by a mystical experience project their fantasies on such experiences. But they aren't veridical; they tell us what's inside, not what's out there. But there's another kind of reverence—a wholehearted devotion to the splendor of biological diversity, the magnificence of nature, and the promise of humanity. I don't stand in awe of a deity, but my loyalty to what's of greatest worth recalls the Old English "weorthscipe" (worth-ship) which is the root of "worship." Devotion and commitment can be misplaced and mishandled. But with appropriate discrimination and judgment, I can avoid modern superstitions and idolatries. Therefore, I call for a "discerning reverence."

B. The Humanist as Activist: Foresight Calls Forth Humane Actions

I seek practical ways to move individuals and organizations from where they are now to where they must be if ever the human species is to reach its full potential. I do this by focusing on personal growth as well as broad political alliances.

4. Who am I? I naturally identify with my children and loved ones: what happens to them happens to me! As I mature spiritually, I enlarge that circle to encompass people I'll never meet, contemporaries on the other side of the globe or generations that'll live in some distant future. I can go further: all life forms on the planet form my indispensable body, even as the planet is my unique home. I must organize with others in such a way that humanity continues to exist on a hospitable planet; otherwise, all our causes will be short lived. I'm a Starchild—all life on the planet, my veritable body; humanity, past and future, my identity; the Earth, my home; the Sun, my creator. With others I must form institutional alliances to safeguard the future well being of the species. We all cooperate or we all die prematurely. Humanity is one.

5. What am I Doing? Every day I add another page to a book called "My Life."

I do this with my actions. As I survey this book, I accept the fact that what has been written cannot be erased: what I'm proud of or ashamed of. What counts are the empty pages that I'll fill from now on. I create the meanings of my life through the purposes I pursue. Will my life story be a self-serving soap opera or a story with a little class? It's up to me.

6. What Inspires My Actions? Ennobling stories—religious and secular—evoke my larger self and bring out the best in me. Certainly, black humor and satire are crucial in combating cant and sentimentality. In addition to stories, I'm indebted to people who've shown me what I'm capable of. As a rabbi once said: "If not me, who? If not now, when?" I add, "Am I acting now as I'd want others to act?"

C. The Humanist as Detective: Curiosity Calls Forth Intellectual Integrity

Since no necessary connection exists between my life stance and my worldview, I honor no taboos in investigating how the world works, what happened in history, and posing hard questions to those who make outrageous claims. Everything must be transparent. Nothing is exempt from scrutiny.

7. What's So? In explaining how the world works, I rely on the naturalist project that guides scientific communities. I refer to research programs as "projects" because they're still in the works. Methodological naturalism is open-minded and open-ended, whereas metaphysical naturalism is dogmatic and unnecessary. The God of the gaps—importing a God to explain something scientists haven't yet explained—will die a slow and natural death without our declaring a funeral service prematurely. This formulation sidesteps issues raised by science studies programs.

8. What Happened? When historians narrate history, they insist on a single standard. It applies to someone working on a family history, elated to find royalty, but dismayed to find horse thieves. It applies to a nation happy to flaunt past policies that are admirable, but eager to wallpaper over dubious actions. It applies to a religion that focuses on its saints or heroes, but hides charlatans and shady characters in its past. The task of laying out what happened in the past can't be determined by what a powerful community wants today. This formulation sidesteps issues raised by postmodernists.

9. What's Credible? In assessing the claims made by philosophers and theologians, I use the laugh test. Tact is required. On the one hand, it won't do to imply they're lacking in honesty, intelligence, or courage. That's no way to open minds or win allies. On the other hand, I can't ignore valid critiques of theism. To avoid getting stuck at this intellectual level, I dealt with attitudes and actions in sections A and B first.

My Personal Credo. Eventually I'll die, as will humanity and all life forms in the cosmos. This transient nature of reality doesn't diminish my veneration of humanity's promise. May my species reach its natural lifespan and promote humane values in the interval!

And a final post-script:

A suggested improvement for the question on dogmatism. Instead of a modern version of resurrection try this:

Recently *The New York Times* noted that one of the medical journals had published an article about a double-blind experiment with the usual controls that indicated people who were prayed for . . . were cured at a faster rate than those who hadn't received prayers. The first response was from other researchers who wondered if there were flaws in the experimental design, the second response was from some clergy who scorned the dogmatism of researchers who had doubted the validity of the initial experiment, and the third response was to ask for others to replicate the issue with improved design. Which response comes closest to your reaction?

I didn't list the natural fourth response: Was the original journal article dated April 1? The issue is the one raised by David Hume: the greater the deviance from what you'd normally expect, the greater must be the effort to find out if there are other explanations. Much on the order of an astronaut who claims he has some dust that smells like cheese—something he picked up on the moon.

7. MARK THOMAS, PRESIDENT, ATHEISTS OF SILICON VALLEY

Thank you for the no-doubt significant effort in writing the survey questions, and collating and analyzing the data. Although the sample of Atheists is obviously limited, I hope that our responses will give you insights into a worldview that is held by millions of Americans and others worldwide.

I found it interesting that you found a low percentage of Atheists had a "religious upbringing." It's been my experience that the "amazing apostates" can be quite strong about their Atheism, after rejecting religion. You noted that most (76 percent) of the respondents said they had once been more religious; most of my Catholic friends in high school turned Atheist in college or before.

For me an important catalyst into stronger Atheism was the web, especially Internet Infidels.

Your insight into the difficulty of the journey to non-belief was good. Those raised in more fundamentalist religions often experienced real mental pain and anxiety, in addition to family problems, during the process of removing the religion engrams from their minds. Part of the good that Atheist groups can do is helping these people realize that there's nothing wrong with them.

Again, thank you.

8. DICK HEWETSON, GAY AND LESBIAN ATHEISTS AND HUMANISTS OF SAN FRANCISCO

Thank you for doing the survey. The number of participants (and many of us belong to more than one of the groups) was encouraging.

I doubt as you comment that the number of persons with Jewish backgrounds may have been over-represented in this study. I am 74 years old and have found that most of my Jewish friends both here and in the Midwest (Minnesota and Wisconsin) are nonbelievers. Although they tend to identify as Jewish, they are not observant followers of Judaism. Some attend high holy days as part of their "culture" but do not believe in god. Rabbi Sherwin Wine who founded Jewish Humanism has said that the "holocaust proved to most Jews that god does not exist." Every non-theistic group I belong to has had a large percentage of Jewish members.

As a gay male, I am often asked by my non-believing friends why so many gay folks are Christians. I do not have an answer. It amazes me that gay people can adhere to monotheistic religions which have persecuted them for centuries. (This would be an interesting survey.)

Often in your narrative you refer to our beliefs. For most of us we claim that we do not have beliefs. We are nonbelievers which you also say. It is only because most people are believers or theists that we must identify ourselves.

Thanks again for a wonderful project. I hope it brings you many rewards. They are deserved.

NOTES

1. We also sent the chapters and the same request to our contacts in Alabama and Idaho, but did not receive any response.

2. The Garrison-Martineau Project was founded by Chris Lindstrom to open channels of communication between atheists and those who believe in God. Small groups often composed of atheists, liberal believers, and fundamentalists meet to explain themselves to one another, often with interesting results and even "Ah-Ha!" experiences. You can find out more at http://www.garrisonmartineau.com.

3. We appreciated this suggestion and substantially reworked chapter 9.

SURVEY SENT TO THE SAN FRANCISCO ATHEISTS CLUBS

A. *People have different concepts of "God." Do you believe in a supernatural power, a deity:*

That is a thinking, self-aware being, not just some physical force like the "Big Bang."   ___ No ___ Yes

That is almighty, can do anything it decides to do?   ___ No ___ Yes

That is eternal: always was, and always will be?   ___ No ___ Yes

That intentionally created the universe for its own purposes?   ___ No ___ Yes

That is constantly aware of our individual lives and hears our prayers?   ___ No ___ Yes

That is all-loving and all-good?   ___ No ___ Yes

That will judge us after we die, sending some to Heaven and others to Hell?   ___ No ___ Yes

B. *Assume the descriptions above comprise the "traditional" concept of God in our culture. Do you believe in it?*

___ I am an **atheist**. I do not believe in the existence of this "traditional" God. I believe it does *not* exist.

___ I am an **agnostic**. I do not believe in the existence of this "traditional" God, *nor* do I disbelieve in it.

___ I am a **theist**. I believe in the existence of this "traditional" God.

Elaboration: What name/term do you personally prefer to use to describe yourself (e.g. humanist, atheist, non-believer, un-believer, non-theist, heretic)? _____

C. If you do not believe in the "traditional" God, *is there any sense in which you do believe in "God"*? If so, would you please describe what kind of God or supernatural being or supernatural force that you DO believe in?

Does this being play an active role in human lives? (If so, how?)

D. *To what extent did you have a "religious upbringing"?* That is, to what extent, adding it all up, did the important people in your life—such as your parents, teachers, and church officials (if any)—do the following as you were growing up?

    0 = To no extent at all
    1 = To a slight extent
    2 = To a mild extent
    3 = To a moderate extent
    4 = To an appreciable extent
    5 = To a considerable extent
    6 = To a great extent

_____ 1. Emphasize attending religious services as acts of personal devotion?

_____ 2. Review the teachings of the religion at home?

_____ 3. Make religion the center, the most important part of your life?

_____ 4. Emphasize that you should read scriptures or other religious materials?

_____ 5. Discuss moral "dos" and "don'ts" in religious terms?

_____ 6. Make it clear that about the worst thing you could do in life would be to abandon your religion?

_____ 7. Stress being a good representative of your faith, who acted the way a devout member of your religion was expected to act?

_____ 8. Teach you that your religion's rules about morality were absolutely right, not to be questioned?

_____ 9. Tell you how wonderful it would be in heaven for all eternity?

_____ 10. Teach you that your religion was the truest religion, closest to God?

_____ 11. Stress that it was your responsibility to fight Satan all your life?

_____ 12. Impress upon you that unrepentant sinners would burn in hell for all eternity?

_____ 13. Make religion relevant to almost all aspects of your life?

_____ 14. Tell you how wrong it was to sin against a loving God?

_____ 15. Have you pray before bedtime?

_____ 16. Teach you to *strictly* obey the commandments of almighty God?

_____ 17. Teach you that persons who tried to change the meaning of scripture and religious laws were evil and doing the devil's work?

_____ 18. Get you to do many "extra" religious acts so that the family religion "filled your life"?

_____ 19. Make a personal commitment to God as your only hope and savior?

_____ 20. Teach you to obey the persons who acted as God's representatives, such as priests, ministers or rabbis?

E.

1. *In what religion, if any, were you raised?* (e.g., Baptist, Episcopalian, Hindu, etc.)

_____

2. Was either of your parents an atheist or an agnostic? (Circle if so) Father Mother

3. Was any of your grandparents an atheist
or an agnostic?   None One Two Three Four

F.

1. *Do you presently consider yourself a member of an organized religion,* or associated with one in some way?

2. If so, what religion (e.g., Catholic, Lutheran, Judaism, etc.)?

_____

3. How often do you attend church in an average month? _____ times in an average month.

G. *To what extent did doubts* about each of the following affect you and lead you to your current viewpoint on religion? That is, to what extent have you had doubts about religion, serious concerns about the basic truth of religion, because of the following?

    0 = To no extent at all
    1 = To a slight extent
    2 = To a mild extent
    3 = To a moderate extent
    4 = To an appreciable extent

5 = To a considerable extent
6 = To a great extent

_____ 1. The existence of God, an all-good, all-powerful supreme being who created the universe.

_____ 2. The problem of evil and unfair suffering in the world.

_____ 3. The history of religion; bad things religions did in the past.

_____ 4. Evolution vs. Creation.

_____ 5. The way religious people sometimes pressured others to believe what they believe.

_____ 6. The hypocrisy of "religious" people (i.e., the nonreligious behaviour of supposedly religious people).

_____ 7. Getting to know people from other religions, or people with no religion.

_____ 8. The death of a loved one.

_____ 9. Religious teachings about sex.

_____ 10. The way some religious people seemed interested mainly in getting money from others.

_____ 11. The intolerance some religious people showed toward other religions.

_____ 12. Religious teachings about the role of women.

_____ 13. Threats about what would happen if you were bad (e.g., being condemned to hell).

_____ 14. Finding that being religious did not bring peace and joy after all.

_____ 15. The intolerance some religious people showed toward certain other people (e.g., homosexuals).

_____ 16. Claims that the Bible is the word of God.

_____ 17. The way religion kept people from enjoying themselves in sensible ways.

_____ 18. Religious teachings often did not make sense; they seemed contradictory, or unbelievable.

_____ 19. What happens to us when we die? Is there really an afterlife?

_____ 20. Religious faith made people "blind," not questioning teachings that should be questioned.

H. *How, in your own words, did you reach your present beliefs about God and religion?*

1a. Was there a time when you were much more religious than you are now? No Yes

b. When? For how long?

c. At about what age did *serious* doubts begin to occur?

d. Do you remember a particular belief, or experience, being involved?

2a. Did you ask anyone, such as your parents or a teacher/minister, for help in dealing with these doubts? Who?

b. If so, what was their response?

c. Did this help?

d. Did you talk with anyone else, or read things, to help you decide?

e. What finally decided the matter for you?

3. How old were you when you decided you were an atheist or an agnostic, *if* you've decided you are? _____

4a. What has your lack of religious faith cost you? Did it put a strain between you and your relatives or friends?

b. Have you paid some price for your views on religion in other ways? Please explain.

5. Suppose a teenager came to you for advice about religion. S/he had been raised a Christian, and religion had played a big part in how s/he had been raised. But now this person is having questions about that religion, and wants your advice on what to do.

a. What would you say?

b. Would you want this person to end up believing what you believe?

c. Would you try to lead them to share your beliefs?

I. Please give your reactions to each of the statements below, according to the following scale:

-4 = Very strong disagreement
-3 = Strong disagreement
-2 = Moderate disagreement
-1 = Slight disagreement
 0 = Neutral or no opinion
+1 = Slight agreement
+2 = Moderate agreement

+3 = Strong agreement
+4 = Very strong agreement

_____ 1. Anyone who is honestly and truly seeking the truth will end up believing what I believe.

_____ 2. There are so many things we have not discovered yet, nobody should be absolutely certain his beliefs are right.

_____ 3. The things I believe in are so completely true, I could never doubt them.

_____ 4. I have never discovered a system of beliefs that explains everything to my satisfaction.

_____ 5. It is best to be open to all possibilities, and ready to reevaluate all your beliefs.

_____ 6. My opinions are right, and will stand the test of time.

_____ 7. Flexibility is a real virtue in thinking, since you may well be wrong.

_____ 8. My opinions and beliefs fit together perfectly to make a crystal-clear "picture" of things.

_____ 9. There are no discoveries or facts that could possibly make me change my mind about the things that matter most in life.

_____ 10. I am a long way from reaching final conclusions about the central issues in life.

_____ 11. The person who is absolutely certain she has the truth will probably never find it.

_____ 12. I am absolutely certain that my ideas about the fundamental issues in life are correct.

_____ 13. The people who disagree with me may well turn out to be right.

_____ 14. I am so sure I am right about the important things in life, there is no evidence that could convince me otherwise.

_____ 15. If you are "open-minded" about the most important things in life, you will probably reach the wrong conclusions.

_____ 16. Twenty years from now, some of my opinions about the important things in life will probably have changed.

_____ 17. "Flexibility in thinking" is another name for being "wishy-washy."

_____ 18. No one knows all the essential truths about the central issues in life.

_____ 19. Someday I will probably realize my present ideas about the BIG issues are wrong.

_____ 20. People who disagree with me are just plain wrong, and often evil as well.

_____

_____

_____ 21. Jesus of Nazareth was divine, the Son of God.

_____

_____

_____ 22. I would not mind if my child had devoutly religious teachers in elementary school.

_____ 23. All people may be entitled to their own religious beliefs, but I don't want to associate with people whose views are quite different from my own.

_____ 24. I would not mind at all if my son's best friends were all highly religious.

_____ 25. If a politician were deeply religious, I would refuse to vote for him even if I agreed with all his other ideas.

_____ 26. It would not bother me if my children regularly went to some religion's "youth group" with their friends.

_____ 27. If it were possible, I'd rather have a job where I worked with people with the same views about religion that I have, rather than with people with different views.

_____ 28. I have personally been discriminated against because of my nonreligious beliefs.

_____ 29. In general, people with my nonreligious beliefs are discriminated against in our society.

J. Suppose a law were passed requiring strenuous teaching in public schools *against* belief in God and religion. Beginning in kindergarten, all children would be taught that belief in God is unsupported by logic and science, and that traditional religions are based on unreliable scriptures and outdated principles. All children would eventually be encouraged to become atheists or agnostics. How would you react to such a law?

_____ I think this would be a *bad* law. No particular kind of religious beliefs should be taught in public schools.

_____ I think this would be a *good* law. These particular beliefs should be taught in public schools.

K. Suppose that next month a group of archeologists working in the Near East announce the discovery of a group of ancient parchments very similar to the famous Dead Sea Scrolls in a Syrian cave. Radiocarbon dating establishes that the inscriptions were made on parchment between 25 and 50 CE/AD. The language is plainly classical Latin, and the scrolls are quite clearly the "file" that the Romans compiled on Jesus of Nazareth. They establish that Jesus, a carpenter's son of Joseph and Mary from Nazareth, began to preach in present-day Palestine when he was 30, claiming to be the Messiah. Witnesses, including spies sent by the occupying Romans, confirm the miracles reported in the New Testament. Specifically, Jesus turned ordinary water into wine, walked upon water, multiplied loaves and fishes, raised Lazarus to life, and cured scores of people of many serious illnesses. The Roman officials, it is clear from the file, were plainly skeptical of these stories, but painstaking and detailed examination of the evidence could not discredit it and left them very worried and puzzled.

They decided, therefore, to put Jesus to death, fearing he was the Messiah who would overthrow their rule. After the crucifixion, Pontius Pilate made sure Jesus was dead, according to the records, and posted soldiers at the tomb to make sure the body stayed inside. The guards testified that they periodically rolled aside the stone to make sure Jesus' body was exactly as it should be, and the body was unquestionably dead. Then, the guards said, after several days a very bright light suddenly burst from the tomb, the rock fell away, and a very alive and radiant Jesus emerged and spoke to them. The file then contains many reports that Jesus was seen for several weeks thereafter in various parts of Palestine and then disappeared. Pontius Pilate, fearing for his position if the story ever reached Rome, ordered the file destroyed and the followers of Jesus persecuted. But instead the file was apparently hidden, then lost until now.

Other scholars examine the scrolls and eventually pronounce them genuine and unaltered in any way. In short, there apparently was a Jesus of Nazareth, and the story of the Gospels is confirmed by records kept by the government at the time.

Now this story is not true. It is entirely hypothetical. But imagine for the sake of the following question that the discovery and conclusions *described above actually occurred. How would you* then *respond to the following question, on the -4 to +4 scale you used on the last page?*

_____ Jesus of Nazareth was divine, the Son of God.

L. What would be required, what would have to happen, for you to believe in the "traditional" God described in "A" at the beginning of this survey? Are there conceivable events, or evidence, that would lead you to believe? What, for example?

M. Some people cannot accept traditional religious teachings because they require an act of faith. They base their beliefs instead on logic and science. Would you now indicate to what extent *logic and science* bring you **happiness, joy and comfort** in each of the following ways?

0 = To no extent at all
1 = To a slight extent
2 = To a mild extent
3 = To a moderate extent
4 = To an appreciable extent
5 = To a considerable extent
6 = To a great extent

_____ 1. They tell me the purpose of my life. (How much happiness, joy and comfort have logic and science given you through their explanation of the purpose of your life?)

_____ 2. They provide the surest path we have to the truth.

_____ 3. They help me deal with personal pain and suffering.

_____ 4. They enable me to work out my own beliefs and philosophy of life.

_____ 5. They take away fear of dying.

_____ 6. They enable me to search for the truth, instead of just memorizing what others say.

_____ 7. They tell me what is right and wrong.

_____ 8. They serve as a check on my own biases and wrong ideas.

_____ 9. They provide an anchor in my life that keeps me from going astray.

_____ 10. They explain the mysteries of life.

_____ 11. They help me control evil impulses.

_____ 12. They have provided satisfying answers to all the questions in life.

_____ 13. They make me feel safe.

_____ 14. They bring me the joy of discovery.

_____ 15. They reveal how I can live a happy life.

_____ 16. They give the satisfaction of knowing that my beliefs are based upon objective facts and logic, not an act of faith.

N. Many people find great comfort in religion. It tells them the purpose of their lives. It helps them deal with pain and suffering. It lessens their fear of death, and indeed promises them life eternal. It tells them what is right and wrong. It provides an anchor, and explains mysteries, and makes them feel safe. And it seems to pay off in various ways. For example, several well-controlled studies have found that, on the average, persons who attend church frequently live longer than those who do not.

If you are an atheist or an agnostic, you probably realized all or most of this long ago. And yet you turn your back on all these benefits. Why? What makes your position so worthwhile that you give up all this? Why can't you believe what most people find it very natural and easy to believe?

O. *Spouse*: Are you presently married, or do you presently have a long-term partner? ___ No ___ Yes

If so, is your partner an atheist? __ agnostic? __ believer in traditional God? Other:

_____

How often does your partner attend church in an average month? _____ times in an average month.

P. *Children*: To what extent would you want your children to have the same religious beliefs that you have?

____ I would stress my point of view as they were growing up, trying to get them to adopt my views.

____ I would want them to make up their own minds, but I would *not* make religion an important issue. I would not pressure them to believe as I do, *nor* would I purposely have them exposed to traditional teachings.

____ I would want them to make up their own minds, and I *would* try to make it an important issue in their lives. I would try to get them to seriously examine many different points of view on religion.

____ I would see to it they received a strong traditional religious education, and hope they accepted those beliefs.

Other: _____

Q. Imagine for the sake of argument that you have a "Hidden Observer" in you, which knows your every thought and deed, but which only speaks when it is safe to do so, and when directly spoken to. This question is for your Hidden Observer. "Does this person (that is, you) have *doubts about her/his "public" stand* on the existence of God? Does this person actually believe that the traditional God of Judeo-Christian religions really exists?

_____ Yes (s)he has secret doubts about her/his "public" stand on the existence of God, which (s)he has kept strictly to herself/himself.

_____ Yes, (s)he has doubts about her/his "public stand," but others (such as parents or friends) know (s)he has these doubts.

_____ No, (s)he totally believes her/his "public" stand.

_____ Other: _____

R. Please rate your *overall attitude toward* the groups below, using the "evaluation thermometer" printed to the right. If you have a favorable attitude toward a specific group, you would indicate a score somewhere between 50 degrees and 100 degrees, depending on how favorable your evaluation is of that group. On the other hand, if you have an *un*favorable attitude toward a specific group, you could give them a score somewhere between 0 degrees and 50 degrees, depending on how *un*favorable your evaluation is of that group. The labels provided will help you to locate your rating on the thermometer. However, you are *not* restricted to the numbers indicated—feel free to use any number between 0 degrees and 100 degrees.

100 Extremely favorable
90 Very favorable
80 Quite favorable
70 Fairly favorable
60 Slightly favorable
50 Neither favorable
nor unfavorable
40 Slightly unfavorable
30 Fairly unfavorable
20 Quite unfavorable
10 Very unfavorable
0 Extremely unfavorable

1. ____ Christians

2. ____ Christian fundamentalists

3. ____ People who believe in a "traditional" God

4. ____ Atheists

5. ____ Hindus

6. ____ People who are not sure, one way or the other, whether the "traditional" God exists

7. ____ Jews

8. ____ Jewish fundamentalists

9. ____ Muslims

10. ____ Muslim fundamentalists

S. 1. Your gender is: Female Male

2. Your age is: ____ years.

3. Years of formal education completed:

8   9   10   11   12   13   14   15   16   17   18   19   20   21   22   23   24

4. With which national political party do you usually identify, and vote for?

____ None; uninterested

____ Democrats

___ Republicans

___ Interested but Independent

Other: _____

Thank you very much. Please return this survey in the envelope provided.

INDEX